OUR HOLY TREASURE
Devotions For Life

Charles W Morris

Copyright © 2024 Charles W Morris

All rights reserved. No part of this book may be used or reproduced by any means, graphic, electronic, or mechanical, including photocopying, recording, taping, or by any information storage retrieval system without the written permission of the publisher except in the case of brief quotations embodied in critical articles and reviews.

Scriptures are taken by permission from the English Standard Version of the Bible

Books may be ordered through booksellers or by contacting:
RSIP
Raising the Standard International Publishing L. L. C.
https://www.rsipublishing.com

RSIP-Charles Morris
https://www.rsiministry.com
Navarre, Florida

ISBN 9781960641434

Printed in the United States of America
Edition Date: January 2024

CONTENTS

1	Building God's Kingdom Or Man's Warehouse	1
2	The Counsel Of The Righteous	3
3	Our Holy Treasure	5
4	Cleanse Me	7
5	Godly Dental Checkup	9
6	Imitating His Passion	11
7	Unity Of The Brethren	13
8	Our Ways Versus God's Ways	15
9	Keeping God's Commandments	17
10	Walking In Victory	19
11	Who Are We Walking With Tomorrow?	21
12	Arrogance Versus Humility	23
13	The Power Of The Tongue To Bless Or Curse	25
14	The Lord's Messengers	27
15	The House Of God	29
16	Asking A Hard Thing	31
17	God Still Used Balaam	33
18	How Can We Enter Into The Rest Of The Lord?	35
19	Obeying God's Commands Part 1	37
20	Obeying God's Commands Part 2	39
21	A New Beginning Of Obedience To God	41
22	What's In A Name Part 1	44
23	What's In A Name Part 2	47

24	What's In A Name Part 3	50
25	Deliverance From The Power Of Sin	53
26	What Brings About Change?	55
27	Developing God-Awareness	57
28	Standing Before God	59
29	The Fear Of Death	61
30	I Can't Go Back	63
31	Focused On His Suffering	66
32	No Fellowship With Natural Things	68
33	Revealed Revelation	70
34	Do Not Touch The Holy Things	72
35	No More Superstars	75
36	Interceding In The Spirit Part 1	77
37	Interceding In The Spirit Part 2	79
38	In Christ: A New Man, Yet A Child	81
39	Temple Of The Most High	83
40	Our Sentence Of Death	85
41	The Root Of The Natural Man	87
42	The Divine Nature	89
43	Willing To Be Made Willing	91
44	Behind The Veil	93
45	Cultivating The Fallow Ground	95
46	Answered Prayers	97
47	Travailing: Love In Action	99
48	Kingdom Giving	102

49	A Covenant Of Ritual Or A Covenant Of Reality	105
50	Foreknown By The Father	107
51	Predestined By The Father	109
52	Called By The Father	111
53	Justified By The Father	113
54	Glorified By The Father	115
55	Our Spiritual Growth	117
56	A Faith That Works	119
57	Drawing Near To The Father	122
58	Love One Another	125
59	Believers Should Not Hurt One Another	127
60	Love Your Enemies	130
	More Books By Charles Morris	133
	About The Author	135

-1-
BUILDING GOD´S KINGDOM OR MAN´S WAREHOUSE?

Matthew 6:20-21 (ESV) but lay up for yourselves treasures in heaven, where neither moth nor rust destroys and where thieves do not break in and steal. 21 For where your treasure is, there your heart will be also.

Working on a job can easily overwhelm our priorities. We can lose our focus on God by simply focusing on the end result and not our job(s) to do in between. It is easy to fall into the "I am busy" mentality and not devote time to fellowship and family. Meanwhile, we make excuses that somehow our "next" promotion will buy us happiness while our families at home are yearning for attention and our important relationships fall by the waist side.

God knows what we all need to provide and care for our families (including the temptations we all face). 1 John 3:16 says that because of the love of God, Jesus chose to lay his life down for us so we can do so likewise and spend time building up our brethren. This way, our treasure can be shared with others, and the Kingdom of God is advanced.

Have you noticed the people who take time for you are usually the ones you also want to keep sharing with over time? Be that person who has time for others and has a heart for the things of God. The person who does not make time for others, only thinking of himself, closes the door to the Kingdom of God and opens the door spoken of in Matthew 6:21.

Thought to Ponder:

Our Father in Heaven has time for us when we have time for Him. Let Him touch your heart with joy and good tithings, for the Bible says the Kingdom of God is at hand. It is time to choose between either building a warehouse for yourself or preparing others for the Kingdom to come.

Consider This:

Thank God for your family and Christian brothers and sisters. Ask the Father to show you areas to serve those around you with a heart ready to walk out His vision (personally, within the body of Christ, and nationally).

-2-
THE COUNSEL OF THE RIGHTEOUS

Psalms 1:1-3 (ESV) Blessed is the man who walks not in the counsel of the wicked, nor stands in the way of sinners, nor sits in the seat of scoffers; 2 but his delight is in the law of the LORD, and on his law he meditates day and night. 3 He is like a tree planted by streams of water that yields its fruit in its season, and its leaf does not wither. In all that he does, he prospers.

How often have we said, "What do I do now?" If we let our minds take over while ignoring the things of God, the first thing we will want to do is share our current crisis with every person around us. This practice often leads to gossip and unfruitfulness. Have you ever noticed that mature Christians are usually quiet in the middle of a storm? They are not the ones to try to convince people they are the smartest ones in the room by declaring God´s Truth. Instead, they take on His power by standing on the Word of God and His promises. Those promises that God has made, among other things, are the fact that we are BLESSED by waiting on Him.

God allows people to continue on their track, even if it is not Godly, hoping they might eventually be redeemed. We should disagree with the counsel of complainers, gossipers, mockers, and the lost. We often take on fear after these conversations with those who stand against the promises of God.

Thought to Ponder:

Next time a crisis arises, share it through prayer to God, and if it cannot wait any further, then bring it before the church elders for counsel. Let the sinners keep sinning and resist trying to convince a lost person how much sin he is in. Instead, drink from the quiet waters of the Holy Spirit and be still.

Consider This:

Thank God for His provisions in your current crisis of faith and ask Him to soften your heart to receive His vision for you. If you do not sit with the scoffers, walk with the wicked, and stand with the sinners, you will be like a tree planted by the water and will always prosper.

-3-
OUR HOLY TREASURE

Matthew 7:6 (ESV) "Do not give dogs what is holy, and do not throw your pearls before pigs, lest they trample them underfoot and turn to attack you.

Bless God, for He is HOLY. Our Lord Jesus Christ has made the ultimate sacrifice, forgave our sins, and redeemed us, and we thank Him by wearing our wedding gowns in the mud.

HOLINESS is a pursuit, a thing to treasure, and a place where Jesus is surrounded by His righteousness. The things He touches become as clean as the Master is. Bless God, for He is HOLY!!!

In the same way, we do not openly share our detailed marriage life with the public. People can get a sense of what is going on between a couple only by their facial expressions to each other.

Couples do not share relational things with people who do not care. In the same way, the Scriptures say we are His people in waiting. The things Jesus shares with us and that we experience are precious and should be kept in the secret places of our hearts and not on public display. If people want to know how we are doing, they only need to look at our facial expressions. Anything else will be tried to be used against us by the enemy, and even a wrong look sets the alarms.

God wants to be close to us. The enemy wants you to be separated. Let the Spirit of God, which is in you, judge the spirit of man in another and their willingness to receive the things of God.

Thought to Ponder:

God wants to give something precious. The enemy wants to take, rob, steal, kill, and destroy that which the Father gives you.

Consider This:

Acknowledge to the Father that He is holy and ask Him to cleanse you with the blood of Jesus. He says you are as white as snow after you receive His forgiveness.

-4-
CLEANSE ME

Matthew 8:2 (ESV) And behold, a leper came to him and knelt before him, saying, "Lord, if you will, you can make me clean."

Yes, Lord, I want to worship you, for You alone are Holy. I speak Your words because You have the power to heal me and make me clean forever. Just speak it, Lord, and I will come in agreement with You, and it will be done for Your glory.

All your struggles today may seem like you are steeped in impossible situations, but for God, all things are possible. Here is a man in Matthew 8:2 who, by Jewish law, was UNCLEAN. Yet he came and honored and worshiped the Lord.

I believe this is a great place to start our day. LORD, we want to honor You. Dear believer, make this your theme today. Lord, we present our request to You, and if the requests are according to the Word and the character of our Father, they will be done in the name of Jesus.

I know this may sound easy, but it is an issue of our hearts. As long as we take the things of this world more seriously than the Lord, we cannot come as the leper who was an outcast of society and present our case before the throne of God.

Thought to Ponder:

I do not know about you, but I need healing today, and in the spirit, I declare the righteousness of God and His blood over me today. I believe that the God of Abraham, Isaac, and Jacob lives in heaven and is faithful to those who love him.

Consider This

Lord, deal with my heart. Make me CLEAN. I receive your forgiveness and stand boldly before You, washed pure with the Blood of Jesus. Thank you, Jesus, for touching me today!

-5-
GODLY DENTAL CHECKUP

Psalms 3:7 (ESV) Arise, O LORD! Save me, O my God! For you strike all my enemies on the cheek; you break the teeth of the wicked.

After getting up today and before reviewing what needs to be done over the day, take a minute to allow the Father to rise up in your life. Ask Him to show you the areas that need arising, where He needs to save you, and how you can create a situation where you will look like a fool if God does not show up. Put your faith in Jesus as an overcomer!

Despite everything the enemy is trying to speak to you at this moment, remind him of his future dental work. The current crisis of faith that God is leading you through has been organized by someone who loves you very much. This process of walking peacefully during a crisis is what Jesus did during his ministry despite knowing He would face the cross not many days ahead.

Life, liberty, and servanthood were some of the things that came from Jesus' faithfulness to keep walking and listening to God in spite of what was rumored by the leadership at the time. The high priests of the church in Jesus' time had a form of Godliness but denied His power. The Bible also calls this unbelief and warns against this very much. Let us NOT deny any of His power today!

Thought to ponder:

How is your outward appearance affected by the crisis of the moment? Does this appearance reveal trust in a loving and faithful Father?

Consider This:

Oh Lord, take charge of my life situations and save me from this world and my enemies. Touch the issues of my heart and bring me into a place where I can see and hear you clearly.

-6-
IMITATING HIS PASSION

Matthew 27:50-51 (ESV) And Jesus cried out again with a loud voice and yielded up his spirit. 51 And behold, the curtain of the temple was torn in two, from top to bottom. And the earth shook, and the rocks were split.

Regarding the word passion, the dictionary gives us (among others) the following definition:

1. A powerful emotion, such as love, joy, hatred, or anger.
2. Ardent love.

It is without question that Jesus Christ was driven by His love. This passion He displayed was to do the will of the Father in all things, even unto death. The Father's devoted love was and is to restore His people to make them the worthy bride for the bridegroom, His son Jesus Christ. With his death, Jesus Christ restored the direct communication to the Father, Himself being the High Priest and intercessor for us. The veil was torn, opening the Holy of Holiest to all believers in the Lord Jesus Christ. In all that Jesus did and said, His passion for the people and His obedience to the Father were the things magnificently displayed.

What is our passion? Is it for our car, hobbies, for our wife and children? Or is our devoted love and passion centered on the Father?

I hope you are passionate about everything, but before anything and anybody, you are deeply sincere in your walk with GOD. I pray that your passion is always to seek the will of the Father in your life first, to be a passionate receiver for the things of GOD!

Thought To Ponder:

As you walk through this day, make frequent stops to reflect on the question: Did I first seek the Father's will before I did what I did? Is what I just said something I would have said with Jesus standing right with me? Or did I act out of my flesh?

Consider This:

I pray that you are filled with the passion that comes from Jesus Christ! Read the following passage to get a glimpse of what Jesus wishes for you and all believers.

John 17:8-11 (ESV) For I have given them the words that you gave me, and they have received them and have come to know in truth that I came from you; and they have believed that you sent me. 9 I am praying for them. I am not praying for the world but for those whom you have given me, for they are yours. 10 All mine are yours, and yours are mine, and I am glorified in them. 11 And I am no longer in the world, but they are in the world, and I am coming to you. Holy Father, keep them in your name, which you have given me, that they may be one, even as we are one.

-7-
UNITY OF THE BRETHREN

Psalms 133:1-3 (ESV) A Song of Ascents. Of David. Behold, how good and pleasant it is when brothers dwell in unity! 2 It is like the precious oil on the head, running down on the beard, on the beard of Aaron, running down on the collar of his robes! 3 It is like the dew of Hermon, which falls on the mountains of Zion! For there the LORD has commanded the blessing, life forevermore.

It is in the heart of the Father that we live together in Christian unity. That is, Christian brothers and sisters, young and old, who are, through the Holy Spirit, connected in the unity of the faith. The Word speaks of "dwelling together," meaning we are to share things of our lives, staying together, almost like a marriage, in which two people decide to intertwine their individual two lives.

Such unity is intense, full of harmony, trust, and expressive, like the oil Moses poured over the head of Aaron. The ointment is so thick that we can watch it flow slowly down the beard, the shoulders, and over the body. Everywhere the oil ran down, it left a trace of its presence. The ointment besmeared Aaron's head, almost like the dew on Mount Hermon that descends upon the mountains of Zion. A harmonic picture of the creation of the Lord being figuratively transferred to His highest design, mankind.

Thought To Ponder:

When the dew spreads out all over the place, when the oil disperses, then all things are touched or "besmeared." Such is the unity of the brethren, not only being united among each other but also in accord with their creator. This unity displays believers as;
1. Chosen priests for the holy service to Him.
2. God's sons and daughters who are soaked daily in the overflowing ointment to live together with the ability to do God's will.

Consider This:

The Spirit of God calls us today as much as in the old times to share our lives in unity with our brothers and sisters. Even physical distance loses its effect on the spiritual. So, let us walk in the Spirit, full of His anointing, predestined for the holy service unto our Lord and the community of believers who represent "His family."

Lord, as Psalms 133 proclaims, unity is sweet and pleasant. Make me a bridgebuilder of relationships without compromising Your Word or character. Anoint me with the oil of Your presence and use me to bring Your body together.

Psalms 133:1-3 (ESV) A Song of Ascents. Of David. Behold, how good and pleasant it is when brothers dwell in unity! 2 It is like the precious oil on the head, running down on the beard, on the beard of Aaron, running down on the collar of his robes! 3 It is like the dew of Hermon, which falls on the mountains of Zion! For there the LORD has commanded the blessing, life forevermore.

-8-
OUR WAYS VERSUS GOD'S WAY

Proverbs 3:5-8 (ESV) Trust in the LORD with all your heart, and do not lean on your own understanding. 6 In all your ways acknowledge him, and he will make straight your paths. 7 Be not wise in your own eyes; fear the LORD, and turn away from evil. 8 It will be healing to your flesh and refreshment to your bones.

Proverbs 14:12-14 (ESV) There is a way that seems right to a man, but its end is the way to death. 13 Even in laughter the heart may ache, and the end of joy may be grief. 14 The backslider in heart will be filled with the fruit of his ways, and a good man will be filled with the fruit of his ways.

The Scriptures give us an understanding of God as an envious, caring, providing, and protecting Father. God is the Father who desires His children to participate in His riches, possessions, and glory.

But when we start looking after worldly riches, it is only a matter of time until we put "walking in our own ways" into practice. The moment we stop seeing Jesus as our "first love," we start losing our ground (land) and our growth and knowledge about God's goodness. True satisfaction and fullness can only be received straight from Daddy's heart and table.

Thought To Ponder:

Let us trust God and acknowledge Him in all our ways. He will guide us in all aspects of life if we allow Him to do so. He knows best how we can reach our individual destiny appointed by the Father because He is the origin of our life's plan.

Consider This:

Father, forgive me for the times I abandoned Your way, will, and plans for my life. My flesh desires to do what is right in my own eyes. Holy Spirit, quicken me when I get out of step with You. Guide me into Your paths, for only there will I find Truth. Only there will I see You.

-9-
KEEPING GOD'S COMMANDMENTS

Deuteronomy 5:1 (ESV) And Moses summoned all Israel and said to them, "Hear, O Israel, the statutes and the rules that I speak in your hearing today, and you shall learn them and be careful to do them.

Deuteronomy 28:1-2 (ESV) "And if you faithfully obey the voice of the LORD your God, being careful to do all his commandments that I command you today, the LORD your God will set you high above all the nations of the earth. 2 And all these blessings shall come upon you and overtake you, if you obey the voice of the LORD your God.

Our God and Lord want to encourage us today to hear His quiet voice in this noisy world, listen to it carefully, mind our ways, and keep His Commandments.

I would like to compare listening to the voice of God, keeping His commandments, and receiving God's blessing with a picture of a train. A train travels on a straight path called train tracks, and when it is going to rest, it arrives at the point of destination. The train can only arrive at its destination by using the train tracks. The train cannot be used next to the train tracks but only when it is on the right path. So, it is the same for us Christians. We can only receive the Father's blessing by listening to the voice of our God.

Thought To Ponder:

Let us make sure we listen to our LORD's voice and do what we hear. We do not want to become dull of hearing because we did not obey and were not faithful in what the Lord gave us.

Consider This:

LORD, let us listen to your voice carefully, keep your commandments, and follow as You direct us. Lord, help us to hear Your still and quiet voice even in this noisy world, and help us to act on what You tell us. We want Your rich blessings poured over us.

-10-
WALKING IN VICTORY

John 17:24 (ESV) Father, I desire that they also, whom you have given me, may be with me where I am, to see my glory that you have given me because you loved me before the foundation of the world.

1 John 5:4-5 (ESV) For everyone who has been born of God overcomes the world. And this is the victory that has overcome the world—our faith. 5 Who is it that overcomes the world except the one who believes that Jesus is the Son of God?

Lord Jesus, we have decided to walk in You today, to stay in the place where You are and where we can walk in Your victory, the victory that overcame the world.

The Scriptures above tell us that it is the will of our Lord Jesus Christ that we stay close to Him and that we walk in the place where He is. In order to see the glory that Jesus saw and have the victory He experienced, we have to walk in Him. We must give God the Father permission to manifest Jesus' character in and through us and be willing to live the kind of life that Jesus did. That includes the good times and the times that are not so pleasant.

Thought To Ponder:

Lord, we make a decision today to walk in You and go to the places You want us to go. Therefore, we will walk in Your victory, the victory that overcame the world.

Consider This:

    Let us walk in you again, Lord Jesus, and live as you did on this earth. Release Your victory in us today. We choose to die to ourselves and allow you to manifest Your Holiness in us.

-11-
WHO ARE WE WALKING WITH TODAY?

Psalms 37:5-6 (ESV) Commit your way to the LORD; trust in him, and he will act. 6 He will bring forth your righteousness as the light, and your justice as the noonday.

Psalms 16:11 (ESV) You make known to me the path of life; in your presence there is fullness of joy; at your right hand are pleasures forevermore.

Where does our path lead us today? Let us commit our ways to the Lord. He will show us the right way!

The Psalmist encourages us that the Lord blesses our ways in all things He leads us into. When we suffer under unrighteousness (injustice), His light will break through, and His righteousness will shine forth.

Let us recognize today that our Lord Jesus Christ is for us. And if He is for us, who can stand against us? He is there whether we realize it or not. Whether we recognize His presence or not depends on whether we allow Christ in His proper position as Lord and Master of our daily lives.

Thought To Ponder:

Is Jesus on our side today? Or better yet, are we on His side and walking in His ways? Jesus is with us who are believers! Let us receive this truth! Do we recognize His presence, or are we doing what is right in our own eyes and going our own ways?

Consider This:

Lord, we put our lives and this day in Your hands. Open our hearts so we can see You being close to us and operating Your will in our hearts. Thank you, Lord, that you alone are our hope and a light in our path.

-12-
ARROGANCE VERSUS HUMILITY

Proverbs 6:16-19 (ESV) There are six things that the LORD hates, seven that are an abomination to him: 17 haughty eyes, a lying tongue, and hands that shed innocent blood, 18 a heart that devises wicked plans, feet that make haste to run to evil, 19 a false witness who breathes out lies, and one who sows discord among brothers.

Proverbs 16:18 (ESV) Pride goes before destruction, and a haughty spirit before a fall.

Haughty eyes are an image of our arrogance! Without spiritual weapons, we continuously do what God hates in the first place.

Perhaps you are familiar with the phrases; "I already know" or "I can do it better?" These speak of pride and arrogance.

The Father resists the proud. However, God gives grace to the humble. Humility is the spiritual weapon of God, which He assures us of His grace and victory!

James 4:6 (ESV) But he gives more grace. Therefore it says, "God opposes the proud but gives grace to the humble."

Thought To Ponder:

Here are some examples of today's training on how to humble ourselves in the Lord.

1. I will let everyone finish speaking today without interruption while I listen.
2. I consciously lay down my abilities, experience, and intellect under the authority of God.

Consider This:

Therefore, I will be satisfied seeking the favor of the Father today instead of trying to impress people with what I know or can do.

Lord, we know from Your Word that You resist the proud and give grace to the humble. Forgive me of my pride. Like the Apostle Paul said, Lord, in my flesh I can boast. I pray that my boasting is limited to my Lord Jesus Christ and Him crucified.

-13-
THE POWER OF THE TONGUE TO BLESS AND CURSE

Proverbs 18:21 (ESV) Death and life are in the power of the tongue, and those who love it will eat its fruits.

James 3:3-12 (ESV) If we put bits into the mouths of horses so that they obey us, we guide their whole bodies as well. 4 Look at the ships also: though they are so large and are driven by strong winds, they are guided by a very small rudder wherever the will of the pilot directs.

5 So also the tongue is a small member, yet it boasts of great things. How great a forest is set ablaze by such a small fire! 6 And the tongue is a fire, a world of unrighteousness. The tongue is set among our members, staining the whole body, setting on fire the entire course of life, and set on fire by hell. 7 For every kind of beast and bird, of reptile and sea creature, can be tamed and has been tamed by mankind, 8 but no human being can tame the tongue. It is a restless evil, full of deadly poison.

9 With it we bless our Lord and Father, and with it we curse people who are made in the likeness of God. 10 From the same mouth come blessing and cursing. My brothers, these things ought not to be so. 11 Does a spring pour forth from the same opening both fresh and salt water? 12 Can a fig tree, my brothers, bear olives, or a grapevine produce figs? Neither can a salt pond yield fresh water.

With some of us, it often works like the following: How shall we know what to think before we hear what we say? In other words, some of us engage our tongues before our minds operate. Sometimes, it would be better if we had bitten on our tongues than simply continued speaking. Some of us keep talking until we find something to say. In all of this speaking, we may find ourselves speaking death or curses instead of life and blessings.

God knows the problem of our tongues very well and why it can make us sin rapidly. Remember, out of the mouth speaks the abundance of the heart.

Thought to Ponder:

A philosopher once said. I would only like to hear your message when it withstands the three filters:
1. Kindness,
2. Truth,
3. Necessity!

Consider This:

Father, please make me mindful to control my tongue today. Father, quicken me by Your Spirit if I am about to dishonor You, others, or myself through my tongue.

-14-
THE LORD'S MESSENGERS

2 Kings 2:1 (ESV) Now when the LORD was about to take Elijah up to heaven by a whirlwind, Elijah and Elisha were on their way from Gilgal.

2 Kings 2:14 (ESV) Then he took the cloak of Elijah that had fallen from him and struck the water, saying, "Where is the LORD, the God of Elijah?" And when he had struck the water, the water was parted to the one side and to the other, and Elisha went over.

Hallelujah, our Lord has spoken! The Father uses many ways to talk to us. In my book "Fifteen Ways To Hear The Voice Of God," I outline the various methods our Lord speaks to His people. In this case, the older prophet passed the prophetic mantel to the younger prophet. Elijah, the man of God, is about to witness and experience his supernatural transport to heaven.

As we read the Old Testament accounts of our Lord speaking, I believe the Scriptures teach we can hear from God today.

Has the Lord spoken to you in a way that leads you to something that you usually would not have done? We must all learn to hear the Father's voice over all the other voices screaming for our attention.

The Lord's voice is always supernatural, even when it comes by way of one of His messengers. His voice should come to us through the Sunday sermon. However, our opportunity to act on the Lord's Words has a time limit! Yes, when we wait too long to obey God's Words, the "window of opportunity" passes from us.

Can you imagine how Elijah felt when the Lord told him he was about to be taken to heaven in a whirlwind? Maybe some of you are feeling expectation and anticipation today.

Thought To Ponder:

Our Lord has previously spoken to us through His Word or one of the other 14 different ways in which He communicates to mankind. Will we obey his commands or wait too long in order to act upon His truth and miss the "whirlwind"? Elijah had a vision and a word from God. We need to study from God's Word how to get plugged into and recognize the Lord's voice so that we fail to hear Him and deny His power and will for us. Elijah walked in God's power and was a channel to release it to others.

Consider This:

Lord Jesus, may we be holy and pure for Your Kingdom. We come against the sin in our lives and plead the blood of Jesus over it. Guide us to the place of destiny you have prepared for us since the beginning of time. Let us take a step closer to our calling today. We release control to You, Lord Jesus! AMEN!

-15-
THE HOUSE OF GOD

2 Kings 2:2-4 (ESV) And Elijah said to Elisha, "Please stay here, for the LORD has sent me as far as Bethel." But Elisha said, "As the LORD lives, and as you yourself live, I will not leave you." So they went down to Bethel. 3 And the sons of the prophets who were in Bethel came out to Elisha and said to him, "Do you know that today the LORD will take away your master from over you?" And he said, "Yes, I know it; keep quiet." 4 Elijah said to him, "Elisha, please stay here, for the LORD has sent me to Jericho." But he said, "As the LORD lives, and as you yourself live, I will not leave you." So they came to Jericho.

I pray you have moved beyond your current "crisis of faith" and found your victory in our Lord Jesus Christ. Our heavenly Father is on the move and ready to bring you to The House of God and The City of Supernatural Victory.

We are looking at studying 2 Kings 2:2-4 although it would be helpful for you to read the entire chapter. In 2:3, I find it very interesting that God sent Elijah on the eve of a great supernatural event to Bethel (The House of God).

When the Father prepares us for the supernatural, it originates from The House of God. Every victory we have overcome originated in the heart of the Father. He spoke it before we knew it! So, God took Elisha to The House of God and gave him confirmation (through the prophets) that a supernatural event was about to happen. The Father provides confirmation today for things He speaks to us concerning His plans. God's creation speaks volumes of confirmation of His Word. Just look around.

Elisha took a stand in The House of God and followed the vision. God leads him to the city of Jericho (the place of supernatural victory). We know from God's Word that Jericho is where God led the Israelites to sound the trumpet over the city, and the walls came down.

Thought To Ponder:

God is leading us to our city of victory. We just need to shout the walls down! Victory is ours, and the supernatural comes from our agreement with the Father's Word. If you want to move in victory, I pray you seek out The House of God and discover His supernatural places. We will be required to stand on His Word, believe in Him for what He said He would do, and then the trumpet of victory will sound!

Consider This:

Lord Jesus, we shout yes to Your victory. Put us on the path of the supernatural. Today, we choose to walk where You walk, say what You say, and do what You do. And all for Your glory. Amen!

-16-
ASKING A HARD THING

2 Kings 2:9-10 (ESV) When they had crossed, Elijah said to Elisha, "Ask what I shall do for you, before I am taken from you." And Elisha said, "Please let there be a double portion of your spirit on me." 10 And he said, "You have asked a hard thing; yet, if you see me as I am being taken from you, it shall be so for you, but if you do not see me, it shall not be so."

Have you ever faced a problem that could not be solved? Rejoice! Because our God is able to do all things when we place our little faith in a big God!

Elisha is asking Elijah for his Spirit to be upon him. Have we asked the Father for His Spirit to be upon us today? Because without the Holy Spirit, we cannot reach the place God wants us. It may be hard for some of us to admit that we may have gone too long on our own and in our plans without consulting the Father. It is somehow easy to slip into the habit of self-sufficiency, but it is difficult to break that habit. How about our daily prayer life? Or our need to ask for forgiveness and get right with God?

Elisha knew that he needed to be right with God and his Pastor. Elisha had the strength not to run from what his Pastor said about him. He looked beyond his struggles and realized the only thing he could hold onto was God Himself. So, asking for a double portion of God's Spirit was the only way he knew to lead his people.

Israel was not in a very healthy spiritual position during this time. People were worshiping Baal and forsaking

God to worship false gods. The church was struggling. It took a man who wanted to hold onto the standards of God to bring correction. Elisha was about to do that. The people were full of doubt and unbelief. How much has changed today? When Elisha returned to the prophets, they did not even believe him about what had happened to Elijah. The Word says they kept asking him for permission to search for Elijah until he was ashamed of them. Elisha let the prophets follow their unbelieving heart's desires. God does the same today. If we have a heart of unbelief, He allows us to continue this path until we reach our end.

Thought To Ponder:

Really? Is it not time for change? When will we have a heart of faith and believe in what the Father has spoken? Have we come to our wit's end yet? It is time we get right with God concerning faith and ask Him to do the "hard thing." Lord, we desire for a double portion.

Consider This:

Lord, forgive us where we have unbelief in your power and the Word. We ask you to pour out your Spirit on us so we can stay on the narrow path of righteousness.

-17-
GOD STILL USED BALAAM

Numbers 23:19-20 (ESV) God is not man, that he should lie, or a son of man, that he should change his mind. Has he said, and will he not do it? Or has he spoken, and will he not fulfill it? 20 Behold, I received a command to bless: he has blessed, and I cannot revoke it.

For the backstory, you will need to read Numbers, chapters 22 and 23. At this point in his life, Balaam speaks truthfully the words the Lord has given him to express.

Balaam knew the Lord and was a true prophet of the Lord. He makes clear that God always speaks the truth. If he had fully grasped his prophetic speaking, he could have turned from his wicked ways and fulfilled his desire to die as a righteous man.

Numbers 23:10 (ESV) Who can count the dust of Jacob or number the fourth part of Israel? Let me die the death of the upright, and let my end be like his!"

But because his heart was set on worldly rewards, he eventually became a soothsayer and received the reward of the unrighteous, resulting in his dying by the sword.

Numbers 31:8 (ESV) They killed the kings of Midian with the rest of their slain, Evi, Rekem, Zur, Hur, and Reba, the five kings of Midian. And they also killed Balaam the son of Beor with the sword.

Nevertheless, even though God knew Balaam would turn that way, God used him to speak a mighty blessing over His people, Israel.

Thought To Ponder:

Like Balaam, we have a choice. We can become and stay faithful followers of Christ, or we can sell out, longing for the "riches" of the world. If we do not guard our hearts, we can turn into backsliders, and the Holy Spirit will eventually depart us. We decide daily on our walk with the Father and how we use the gifts God has entrusted to us. The Father is faithful and remains the same. He cannot lie and promises to bless us if we walk with Him in word, deed, and thought.

Consider This:

Lord, You are the God who never changes and is always truthful. We want to be proclaimers of Your Word. Please help us turn away from sin and follow the guidance of the Holy Spirit. Lord, please help us to set our hearts completely towards You to receive Your eternal reward. Amen.

-18-
HOW CAN WE ENTER INTO THE REST OF THE LORD?

Hebrews 4:6-7 (ESV) Since therefore it remains for some to enter it, and those who formerly received the good news failed to enter because of disobedience, 7 again he appoints a certain day, "Today," saying through David so long afterward, in the words already quoted, "Today, if you hear his voice, do not harden your hearts."

Let us live in the "Today" to live every moment of the day in Christ. We must position ourselves to hear the Lord speak and have a soft heart of obedience. Only in obedience to God can we enter into the rest of the Lord. The rest is not found on a particular day but in a person.

According to Hebrews 4:6-7, we are allowed to live in the "today" and hear the Lord's voice if we do not harden our hearts. Observing these things, we rest in the Lord Jesus Christ.

We are not to live in the yesterday. We are to forget those things that are behind us. If not, we would be like people attempting to dive their cars, focused only on the rearview mirror. There is an inevitable disaster awaiting us when doing this. Likewise, we cannot live in the future because we have not been promised tomorrow.

Thought To Ponder:

We are to live in this moment. We are to walk in the Spirit and exercise faith for the NOW. Lord, we choose to listen to Your voice, and we ask You for soft hearts and a willingness to obey to maintain the position of Your rest.

Consider This:

Lord Jesus, we conclude for ourselves today to live in the "today" and, therefore, in the moment. Lord, we decide to listen and obey Your voice today. Soften our hearts so that we may understand Your will and act accordingly. Your will be done on earth as it is in heaven.

-19-
OBEYING GOD'S COMMANDS
PART 1

Exodus 20:3-4 (ESV) "You shall have no other gods before me. 4 "You shall not make for yourself a carved image, or any likeness of anything that is in heaven above, or that is in the earth beneath, or that is in the water under the earth.

Our Lord Jesus Christ said, If you love Me, obey my commands.

John 14:15 (ESV) "If you love me, you will keep my commandments.

Loving God and obedience go hand in hand. Obedience to the Father is not a New Testament thing. God has demanded obedience since He created mankind. He gave the Ten Commandments to mankind through Moses as a schoolmaster to reveal that we cannot fulfill the law because of our sinful nature.

Once we come to the Lord Jesus Christ and receive His gift of salvation, we are righteous in our spirit, but our soulish man (thoughts, emotions, and choices) are still messed up. We are in the process of sanctification or being made righteous in our soulish man. Living that righteous life is a life of obedience to the commands of the Father. We can live a righteous life to honor the Father through our testimony.

Why would we look to the Old Testament and the Ten Commandments for guidance? If we are Christians, then according to Romans 6:14, we are no longer under the law but under grace, right? While that is true, it doesn't mean the law was flawed. On the contrary, the law is good, but man is bad. God loved the world enough to give up His Son for us. So, it is still good to observe God's commands, but when we fall short, we receive grace through the work of Jesus on the cross.

With that said, our first two commandments tie in together. We probably aren't worshipping other gods as the Greeks and Romans did, but are we putting other things or activities before God (work, school, games, etc.)? I doubt any of us has an altar set up in our house with an idol on it, but sometimes, when we find a "treasure" at the market, it may be more than a neat-looking keepsake. If we put idols in our homes, even unknowingly, we open a door for darkness into our homes.

Thought To Ponder:

Look around your home to ensure it is cleansed and ready for service to our Lord. We must keep our spiritual eyes open to put the Lord first in our lives and homes.

Consider This:

Lord, please open our eyes and reveal anything in our lives we have put before You and anything in our homes that could be a tool for the enemy. Amen.

-20-
OBEYING GOD'S COMMANDS
PART 2

Exodus 20:16-17 (ESV) "You shall not bear false witness against your neighbor. 17 "You shall not covet your neighbor's house; you shall not covet your neighbor's wife, or his male servant, or his female servant, or his ox, or his donkey, or anything that is your neighbor's."

The first four of the Ten Commandments deal with our relationship with God. The following six deal with our relationship and fellowship with mankind. Exodus 20:16-17 brings it closer to home by instructing us in guidelines concerning our neighbors. Our neighbors don't only apply to the person next door!

We are told not to lie about our neighbor not only because it is not pleasant, and we wouldn't want it done to us, but also because it destroys our reputation and witness. We shouldn't covet because when we do, we are basically saying we aren't happy with what God has blessed us with, and we want more. Covetousness is also tied closely with idolatry. That which we strongly desire becomes an idol we worship. This sin reveals pride issues and is far from the humble servant attitude Jesus teaches us to have.

Thought To Ponder:

Remember the fruit on the tree of knowledge of good and evil that Eve desired. We had a whole garden of perfect fruit that was beautiful and good to eat. But the enemy tempted her to doubt God and His Word into thinking this tree offered her fruit that would make her wiser than anything else she could have consumed. Her desire to be exalted became her downfall. The grass we desire on the other side of the fence might look greener, but according to God's Word, it is a forbidden pasture.

Consider This:

I hope this causes us to examine our hearts and motivates us to evaluate our relationships to maintain purity in word, deed, and thought.

Lord, thank You for providing guidelines so we can know Your boundaries and how we should behave in a Christ-like manner.

-21-
A NEW BEGINNING OF OBEDIENCE TO GOD

REVISITING THE WELCH REVIVAL

Revelation 3:19-20 (ESV) Those whom I love, I reprove and discipline, so be zealous and repent. 20 Behold, I stand at the door and knock. If anyone hears my voice and opens the door, I will come in to him and eat with him, and he with me.

The writing of this devotional came forth because of what God did in February 1904. A great move of God spread across Wales, which is now known as the Welch Revival. However, we must contemplate the ills of Christian complacency and its cure. American evangelist Charles Finney (1792-1875) had this to say about spiritual revival:

"A revival is nothing else than a new beginning of obedience to God."
"Revival comes from heaven when heroic souls enter the conflict determined to win or die-or if need be, to win and die!"

Matthew 11:12 (ESV) From the days of John the Baptist until now the kingdom of heaven has suffered violence, and the violent take it by force.

As many as the Lord loves, He rebukes and chastens. When the Lord rebukes and chastens us, He also commands zealous repentance. Zealous repentance marked the Welch revival. During their revival meetings, the Holy Spirit instructed Evan Roberts to be zealous in these four things:

1. Confession of all known sin.
2. Repentance and restitution.
3. Obedience and surrender to the Holy Spirit.
4. Public confession of Christ.

Thought To Ponder:

The plea of Christ, found above in Revelation 3:20, has been misinterpreted by many. This plea was not meant to be a soul-winning verse misused by pastors and evangelists to get people to open their hearts to Jesus. Revelation 3:20 was meant to show that our Lord is knocking at the door of the church seeking fellowship. It is the Lord seeking to awaken a sleepy, complacent church. As the time for the Master's return draws near, the Lord has called His Church to watch and stay awake.

Mark 13:32-37 (ESV) "But concerning that day or that hour, no one knows, not even the angels in heaven, nor the Son, but only the Father. 33 Be on guard, keep awake. For you do not know when the time will come. 34 It is like a man going on a journey, when he leaves home and puts his servants in charge, each with his work, and commands the doorkeeper to stay awake. 35 Therefore stay awake—for you do not know when the master of the house will come, in the evening, or at midnight, or when the rooster crows, or in the morning— 36 lest he come suddenly and find you asleep. 37 And what I say to you I say to all: Stay awake."

Consider This:

Our Holy Treasure

Lord, bend us and break us. I pray there is less of me and more of thee until there is none of me and all of thee.

-22-
WHAT'S IN A NAME?
PART 1

Psalms 5:11 (ESV) But let all who take refuge in you rejoice; let them ever sing for joy, and spread your protection over them, that those who love your name may exult in you.

What is in a name? William Shakespeare said a rose by any other name is still a rose, and the smell would be just as sweet. The society we live in today does not place considerable significance on people's names and the meaning behind the names. In early Europe, people's last names identified their profession, where they lived, or physical characteristics, such as skin tone.

As an example, take the surname Smith. Smith originally derived from smið or smiþ, the Old English term meaning one who works in metal. The name is related to the word smitan, the Old English form of smite, which also meant "to strike" or hit. It is believed the term "blacksmiths" derived from the surname Smith.

When I tell people my name is Charles, they readily want to call me Charlie or Chuck, and I correct them that my name is Charles. There is nothing wrong with Charlie or Chuck, except they are only abbreviations of who I am. The name Charles was derived from Germany and means "free man."

My last name, Morris, is Irish and English and carries two meanings. The first is Irish and means negro or dark complexion. The skin tone of many in Ireland was fair, with freckles and red hair. However, the Morris family had brown or black hair and a darker skin tone. In this case, the name identified physical characteristics. In England, the name Morris came from the cliffs of Morre and identified a people by where they settled.

Today, many parents pick their child's name after a beloved relative or well-known person. Maybe they choose or create a name because it sounds good and goes well with the last name. Few people really consider the meaning of the names they assign to their children. Names mean something. Names are to reveal the character and purpose of a person.

For example, the name Kenneth is Greek, meaning "to know". Therefore, someone who has the name Kenneth is a seeker of knowledge. The same is true in the names of cities, states, and countries. One of the best-known is the city of Philadelphia in Pennsylvania. The word comes from the Greek words "phileo" (friendship love) and "Delphos" (city). Together, they make "the city of brotherly love."

Jerusalem comes from the Hebrew word "Shalom," meaning "the city of peace." So, even if Shakespeare says that a rose could be called by any other name, we should take names more seriously. In the name, we might discern the nature and character of a person or place.

Thought To Ponder:

This is certainly true of God, which this study is about. We will be looking at a few of the names of God in order to study His character and nature. In our Bible translations, we might only see the word God or Lord, but the Hebrew or Greek word reveals the nature behind the name.

Consider This:

Father, it is such joy learning about Your Name. Teach me as I seek to know the character behind each Name. I want to know Your character, works, and the place You call Your throne. Wow! And all of this is tied to Your name.

-23-
WHAT'S IN A NAME?
PART 2

In this study, we will look at one of the key names for God: Elohim.

Genesis 1:1 (ESV) In the beginning, God created the heavens and the earth.

I am asked many questions about the Bible on many different subjects. One of them is about the Trinity and the different names for God. God reveals Himself throughout eternity by His Name. Each new Name for God indicates another attribute of His wonderful and beautiful nature and character. We can see the believer's growth as we see what name he uses when He addresses our heavenly Father.

As Moses wrote the first five Books in the Bible, we can see His growth and understanding as he uses the different names for God. The first name used for God is in Genesis 1:1. It is the Hebrew word Elohim.

Elohim is a plural word for God. It does not mean that we serve three gods. It means that God is plural within Himself. He manifests Himself as God the Father, God the Son, and God the Holy Spirit. The Hebrew word Elohim is translated as "The All-Powerful One."

The Mormons teach that there is no Holy Spirit, and they corrupt the teaching about God the Father and God the Son. They teach that God is flesh and blood as we are. They are unscriptural in all of their doctrines. They teach that Jesus is the son of God, the same way that I have my sons. This is also a great heresy. God, Elohim (the Father, Son, and the Holy Spirit), always was and had no beginning and will have no end.

Genesis 1:26 (ESV) Then God said, "Let us make man in our image, after our likeness. And let them have dominion over the fish of the sea and over the birds of the heavens and over the livestock and over all the earth and over every creeping thing that creeps on the earth."

Genesia 1:26 is one of the key verses in the Bible for the Trinity and the plurality of God. In it, we see the meaning of Elohim. We see in this verse the statements of "let us," "in our image," and "our likeness." The pagan religions also used the term "Elohim" to speak about their many gods. However, our God, the God of Abraham, Isaac, and Jacob said this in Exodus 20.

Exodus 20:3 (ESV) "You shall have no other gods before me.

Thought To Ponder:

Therefore, the name "Elohim" for our God and the name "elohim" for false pagan gods also gives us an added characteristic for the name. It is the name of a subject to be worshipped. Worship is to "attribute worth" or "bow down." So, anyone or anything worshipped, honored, or revered was considered an Elohim. But the One True God is greater and more majestic than all false gods of mankind. We see through Moses in his statement about the gods of man.

Exodus 18:11 (ESV) Now I know that the LORD is greater than all gods, because in this affair they dealt arrogantly with the people."

The word "gods" in Exodus 18:11 is "elohim" and refers to the false gods of the land.

Consider This:

Father, thank You for Your fullness within Yourself. Thank You that You have revealed Yourself to mankind. Even if we don't fully understand, Lord, we acknowledge that Your name, Elohim, encompasses the Father, Son, and Holy Spirit. You are complete and in You I place my trust.

-24-
WHAT'S IN A NAME?
PART 3

As we have been discussing the names of God, today we will look at El-Elohe and El-Olam.

Genesis 33:20 (ESV) There he erected an altar and called it El-Elohe-Israel.

When we pray or are in dire need, how do we know that our God is able? The answer is in His name. The name "El" represents God, the All-Powerful One. Moses used this name a lot for God in the Scriptures as He saw the great works of our heavenly Father. He recognized that God was all-powerful and there was none other than Him. There are many gods in the world today, to many people. But there is only one El, all-powerful One. He is the Creator of all that is. The Apostle Paul reassured us of this in Ephesians 3:20.

Ephesians 3:20 (ESV) Now to him who is able to do far more abundantly than all that we ask or think, according to the power at work within us,

When the names El-Elohe-Israel are combined, we get "The All-Mighty God of Israel." Now, let's look at the name El-Olam.

Genesis 21:33 (ESV) Abraham planted a tamarisk tree in Beersheba and called there on the name of the LORD, the Everlasting God.

The term "everlasting God" in Genesis 21:33 is "El-Olam." This means that God is our eternal God. He is the Alpha and Omega, the beginning and the end. In Him exists all things.

Thought To Ponder:

Our Lord Jesus Christ did not come into existence in a stable in Bethlehem. He always was, is, and will be. Two thousand years ago, He took on human flesh and dwelt among mankind so that He could die on the cross and pay the price for our sins. The Holy Spirit did not just appear in Acts Chapter 2 on the day of Pentecost. He always existed and was moving on the face of the earth before man was created. Now He comes to dwell within all those who believe in the name of our Lord Jesus Christ.

Genesis 1:2 (ESV) The earth was without form and void, and darkness was over the face of the deep. And the Spirit of God was hovering over the face of the waters.

Consider This:

Father, standing on promise verses like Philippians 4:13 and 4:19 are comforting. We acknowledge, I acknowledge, that I serve an "all-powerful and everlasting God" who can stand behind these promises in truth, might and power.

Philippians 4:13 (ESV) I can do all things through him who strengthens me.

Philippians 4:19-20 (ESV) And my God will supply every need of yours according to his riches in glory in Christ Jesus. 20 To our God and Father be glory forever and ever. Amen.

-25-
DELIVERANCE FROM THE POWER OF SIN

Luke 4:18-19 (ESV) "The Spirit of the Lord is upon me, because he has anointed me to proclaim good news to the poor. He has sent me to proclaim liberty to the captives and recovering of sight to the blind, to set at liberty those who are oppressed, 19 to proclaim the year of the Lord's favor."

Over one-third of the ministry of our Lord Jesus Christ was in the area of deliverance. This is the ministry our Lord gave to the church, the believers that make up the corporate body of Christ. Everywhere our Lord went, He set the captives free. It is time for true believers to rise up and take dominion over the enemy, the power of darkness, and sin.

Much of the sickness, abnormal emotional conditions, nervousness, poverty, and fear are demonic forces turned loose upon Christian believers and the church. The world is filled with problems and is in need of our help. The world has questions but is without answers and hope. We who are saved have hope and the answers to the world's questions.

In Christ, we have the power, authority, and answers to the hurts and fears of our day. The Scriptures warn us about the increased demonic activity in these last days. Therefore, we need to be on guard for our souls as well as the souls of others.

Isaiah 52:1-2 (ESV) Awake, awake, put on your strength, O Zion; put on your beautiful garments, O Jerusalem, the holy city; for there shall no more come into you the uncircumcised and the unclean. 2 Shake yourself from the dust and arise; be seated, O Jerusalem; loose the bonds from your neck, O captive daughter of Zion.

Thought To Ponder:

Our Lord Jesus came to destroy the works of the enemy. God is calling us to take the authority that belongs to us and exercise the victory we have over the works of the enemy.

Consider This:

Father, can we really dare to believe that we have all authority over the enemy and can set the captives free? Father, may it start with me.

-26-
WHAT BRINGS ABOUT CHANGE?

Romans 12:1-2 (ESV) I appeal to you therefore, brothers, by the mercies of God, to present your bodies as a living sacrifice, holy and acceptable to God, which is your spiritual worship. 2 Do not be conformed to this world, but be transformed by the renewal of your mind, that by testing you may discern what is the will of God, what is good and acceptable and perfect.

We have heard that God has changed us in Christ Jesus. But how does that change take place? When we are born again, the Holy Spirit comes to dwell within us, and we are quickened or made alive in our spirit man. However, our soulish man, which is our mind, emotions, and will, is still messed up and needs to change. The Word of God and the Holy Spirit work together to bring about change in our souls.

However, after being saved for several years, it can be emotionally and mentally exhausting to recognize we have remained unchanged in certain areas of our lives.

Change does not happen just because I am a believer. There must be a proactive decision within me to desire change. It is in the Father's heart that I become Christ-like in my actions, thoughts, and speech. Our Lord redeems us in word, deed, and thought.

Thought To Ponder:

In my heart, I need to choose to allow the Father to do this work within me. Here is a quote that is worthy of memorizing. Until a conviction of need exists, there can never be a desire for change. I must see the need for change in my life, emotions, thoughts, and will.

Until a conviction of need exists, there can never be a desire for change.

Consider This:

Father, in every area that you see where I need to change, let me know the need through Your Holy Spirit and Word. In the need that You reveal, give me the strength and courage to change. May Your desire for me to be Christ-like in word, deed, and thought also be my desire, and may it be for Your Glory, Father.

-27-
DEVELOPING GOD-AWARENESS

Colossians 3:2-3 (ESV) Set your minds on things that are above, not on things that are on earth. 3 For you have died, and your life is hidden with Christ in God.

I was born with five senses, which assisted me in developing awareness of my environment. In my flesh, I operate on what I see, feel, taste, hear, and smell. But what sense leads me towards the spiritual environment of becoming sensitive to God-awareness?

Each of my five senses relates to the worldly environment in which I live. I know things and connect to them through touch, smell, sight, hearing, and taste. I know I am alive and well as long as I can relate to my environment through these five senses. But if something happened that I could no longer connect to my environment through these five senses, then most likely, I would be dead, or all quality of life would be lost. Then, death or loss of quality of life is seen as a failure to relate to our environment.

This is basically what happened to Adam when he sinned. Think about it. Adam was innocent and had no concept of sin, right and wrong, or negative thoughts or emotions. His environment was one of perfection, with God walking daily with him.

However, his rebellion and sin brought about spiritual death, resulting in Adam's failure to relate to his current environment in the Garden of Eden. That is why God expelled him from the Garden. Through his rebellion and sin, Adam lost his awareness of God. He was no longer innocent. Adam had become a sinner, and his spiritual senses had died.

Thought To Ponder:

In Christ, we have been given spiritual life and the ability to walk again in God-awareness, having our spiritual eyes opened. In Christ, the relationship between man and God has been restored by faith in the finished work of the cross.

Romans 8:10-11 (ESV) But if Christ is in you, although the body is dead because of sin, the Spirit is life because of righteousness. 11 If the Spirit of him who raised Jesus from the dead dwells in you, he who raised Christ Jesus from the dead will also give life to your mortal bodies through his Spirit who dwells in you.

Consider This:

Father, I desire to be aware of You throughout the day by exercise of my spiritual senses. Help me remember that my environment is that of another world, the unseen spiritual places in you.

-28-
STANDING BEFORE GOD

Hebrews 9:27-28 (ESV) And just as it is appointed for man to die once, and after that comes judgment, 28 so Christ, having been offered once to bear the sins of many, will appear a second time, not to deal with sin but to save those who are eagerly waiting for him.

As a young child, I remember the day I found deep fear in me for the first time. I won't get into the reason behind it, but the fear was so great I felt that my heart was up in my throat. After that, I faced fear many times. By the time I was 18, I had developed deep-seated fears, such as the fear of heights and drowning, just to name a couple. One of my greatest fears was the fear of being alone. I hated loneliness and felt I may remain that way all my life. Of course, all my worries were in the soulish realm related to my five senses. They were fed by my stinking thinking and damaged emotions. However, the one fear I had not faced before was in the spiritual realm that dealt with my eternal destination. That changed in 1974.

The greatest fear of my life came on September 4th, 1974, when I realized I was spiritually lost and headed to a devil's hell. That night, I rolled out of my bed at one in the morning and bowed my knee before God in my room in North Carolina. This was the night I gave my life to the Lord Jesus Christ and received eternal life.

I was a drug addict and a leader of a large group of "friends" who were my party crowd. I remember the intense fear that night of losing all that I knew and entering eternal darkness without God. In the middle of a gathering of friends, I thank God they could not stop me from choosing eternity with Jesus. I cannot even begin to share the joy in my heart as I think of that glorious day when, in the middle of noise and chaos, God was waiting and calling me. I touched life for the first time that night.

Thought To Ponder:

Quote to remember:
We may live in a crowd, but we meet God alone.

Consider This:

Father, help me to remember that within each person is the same loneliness that I felt, even if a world of friends surrounds them. I will love them, Father. Let them know they will stand before You alone, redeemed or eternally judged and condemned. I pray they make the same decision for the Lord Jesus Christ as I made that September morning when you came knocking on the door of my heart.

-29-
THE FEAR OF DEATH

Ephesians 1:3 (ESV) Blessed be the God and Father of our Lord Jesus Christ, who has blessed us in Christ with every spiritual blessing in the heavenly places,

Ephesians 2:4-6 (ESV) But God, being rich in mercy, because of the great love with which he loved us, 5 even when we were dead in our trespasses, made us alive together with Christ—by grace you have been saved— 6 and raised us up with him and seated us with him in the heavenly places in Christ Jesus,

I have met many believers who have been delivered from death but have not been set free from the fear of death.

If I asked ten believers if they were excited about being delivered from the jaws of death and the grave, they would all rejoice and praise God with me with a shout of AMEN. Knowing that we are to dwell in eternity with God the Father and our Lord Jesus Christ is exciting.

What about the fear of death? How many believers are free from that stronghold? Everyone wants to go to heaven, but no one wants to die. We read all the precious truths in the Word that seem so real to us. Why is it, then, if our Lord Jesus Christ conquered death, we are so afraid of it?

It is all a matter of believing in our position with the Father. We have received Christ as our Savior and delivered "from something," but are we afraid to trust Him as Savior "to something"? He has saved me from the power and penalty of sin in this world and will save me from the presence of sin in the world to come.

Thought To Ponder:

We are positioned *with Him* and *in Him*, and He has our best interest in His heart. Death is not a period for the believer, just a comma. We fear death until we see that Jesus took death for us. When we see this, He will win our love and our hearts.

Quote To Remember:
Fear is the absence of God's love. Perfect or mature love casts out ALL FEAR, even the fear of death.

Consider This:

Father, we long to be with you here in Your manifested presence in our personal and corporate times. Make us just as excited about being with you in eternity without the fear of the process known as physical death.

-30-
I CAN'T GO BACK

Isaiah 50:5 (ESV) The Lord GOD has opened my ear, and I was not rebellious; I turned not backward.

Isaiah 50:6-7 (ESV) I gave my back to those who strike, and my cheeks to those who pull out the beard; I hid not my face from disgrace and spitting. 7 But the Lord GOD helps me; therefore I have not been disgraced; therefore I have set my face like a flint, and I know that I shall not be put to shame.

There are many growth areas and stages within the Christian life. But there is a place one can go in the Lord that sets his face like a flint, and in his heart, he settles the issue once and for all. It is the place called *"I can't go back."*

1 Timothy 4:1 (ESV) Now the Spirit expressly says that in later times some will depart from the faith by devoting themselves to deceitful spirits and teachings of demons,

Hebrews 3:12 (ESV) Take care, brothers, lest there be in any of you an evil, unbelieving heart, leading you to fall away from the living God.

From studying the Scriptures, like 1 Timothy 4:1, Hebrews 3:12, Matthew 24:9-13, and many more, we know that many believers will fall away or walk away from the faith. Unfortunately, because of lawlessness, many will backslide and return to the love of the world like they were before salvation.

Matthew 24:9-13 (ESV) "Then they will deliver you up to tribulation and put you to death, and you will be hated by all nations for my name's sake. 10 And then many will fall away and betray one another and hate one another. 11 And many false prophets will arise and lead many astray. 12 And because lawlessness will be increased, the love of many will grow cold. 13 But the one who endures to the end will be saved.

There is a place and a price where we become a disciple of our Lord Jesus Christ, and we know that we can't go back to the world or the ways of the old Adamic nature. I guess it would be suitable for me to describe what our Lord Jesus calls His disciples. I will use Scripture to define the word, and we will see the place and price of setting our face like a flint before the Lord.

Luke 14:26-27 (ESV) "If anyone comes to me and does not hate his own father and mother and wife and children and brothers and sisters, yes, and even his own life, he cannot be my disciple. 27 Whoever does not bear his own cross and come after me cannot be my disciple.

Luke 14:33 (ESV) So therefore, any one of you who does not renounce all that he has cannot be my disciple.

Thought To Ponder:

Why is becoming a disciple so important? When we walk in the manner of a disciple, we are broken and poured out before the Lord. We have turned our backs on the world and the love of temporal things. In doing so, we can have the confession of the Apostle Paul.

Our Holy Treasure

2 Timothy 4:6-7 (ESV) For I am already being poured out as a drink offering, and the time of my departure has come. 7 I have fought the good fight, I have finished the race, I have kept the faith.

Consider This:

Father, this is something that I could not do without You and Your grace. You did not call me to be a victim to the lust of the world and the power of the enemy. You have called me to be victorious. I forsake all and set my face toward You. Give me mercy and grace, and in having done all else, STAND!

-31-
FOCUSED ON HIS SUFFERING

Romans 8:18 (ESV) For I consider that the sufferings of this present time are not worth comparing with the glory that is to be revealed to us.

With so much pain and suffering around us each day, it is difficult sometimes not to be overly focused on it. There is a song by Darrell Evans where he sings,
There's a place where I lose myself in Him.
There's a place where I find myself again.
There's a place where I live to finally die.
There's a place where I lose myself to find.

It sounds like Darrell Evans got a vision of the crucifixion and witnessed each stage of our Lord's death. The movie "The Passion of the Christ" could help us in this. We need to lose ourselves in His suffering and death. We will forget our suffering when it is placed in the suffering and death of our Savior.

There is a cross for each of us to bear, but it cannot be compared to what our Lord did for us. If I want to find myself, then I must lose myself. I must lose even my suffering and pain. If I am to be exalted, then I must be abased. We need to embrace the cross as if Jesus died just for us.

2 Corinthians 4:17-18 (ESV) For this light momentary affliction is preparing for us an eternal weight of glory beyond all comparison, 18 as we look not to the things that are seen but to the things that are unseen. For the things that are seen are transient, but the things that are unseen are eternal.

1 Peter 1:6-7 (ESV) In this you rejoice, though now for a little while, if necessary, you have been grieved by various trials, 7 so that the tested genuineness of your faith—more precious than gold that perishes though it is tested by fire— may be found to result in praise and glory and honor at the revelation of Jesus Christ.

Thought To Ponder:

The Apostle Paul, who certainly was no stranger to trials and tribulations, prayed that we would know the fellowship of His suffering.

Philippians 3:9-11 (ESV) and be found in him, not having a righteousness of my own that comes from the law, but that which comes through faith in Christ, the righteousness from God that depends on faith— 10 that I may know him and the power of his resurrection, and may share his sufferings, becoming like him in his death, 11 that by any means possible I may attain the resurrection from the dead.

Consider This:

Father, I know that pain and suffering are a part of my lot. May I not focus on them but on the suffering my Lord Jesus Christ did on my behalf.

-32-
NO FELLOWSHIP WITH NATURAL THINGS

2 Corinthians 3:14-16 (ESV) But their minds were hardened. For to this day, when they read the old covenant, that same veil remains unlifted, because only through Christ is it taken away. 15 Yes, to this day whenever Moses is read a veil lies over their hearts. 16 But when one turns to the Lord, the veil is removed.

2 Corinthians 4:18 (ESV) as we look not to the things that are seen but to the things that are unseen. For the things that are seen are transient, but the things that are unseen are eternal.

What do I have fellowship with? Another way of asking this would be, What am I comfortable walking hand in hand with? We are, of course, in the world, but we are not of this world. Our fellowship should remain in a world that consists of the Kingdom of God and not of this world.

We only pass through this kingdom until the Father remakes this world and gives the New City from heaven. Our old friends will not understand this type of thinking. We cannot have fellowship with the natural. When I use the term "natural," I am speaking of those who are spiritually lost and those things that are temporary and will one day burn up or fade away. The natural helps to reveal the spiritual, but we are not to fellowship with the natural because light cannot fellowship with darkness.

We are called into fellowship with the Father. Light and darkness cannot exist together, nor can they walk hand in hand together. The Bible instructs us to walk in the Spirit. That means we are to keep in step with the movement and will of the Holy Spirit.

Thought To Ponder:

Not having fellowship with natural things is not a doctrine. Being separated from the world is about the work of Calvary. When the veil of the cross was pulled back, only those with eyes to see would see. We should know that our fellowship is with the Father and the redeemed. Therefore, rejection from the world is to be expected because they cannot accept the things of the Spirit.

1 Corinthians 2:14 (ESV) The natural person does not accept the things of the Spirit of God, for they are folly to him, and he is not able to understand them because they are spiritually discerned.

Consider This:

Father, guard my heart so that I would not receive the ways of the world of the world. I acknowledge that walking in the Spirit is like a fish swimming upstream. It is my choice but not my strength. You have won the battle for me. I am okay walking hand in hand with you and my brothers in the faith. Father, You have taught me that I owe the world and my flesh nothing that would cause me to serve them.

-33-
REVEALED REVELATION

Ephesians 1:16-17 (ESV) I do not cease to give thanks for you, remembering you in my prayers, 17 that the God of our Lord Jesus Christ, the Father of glory, may give you the Spirit of wisdom and of revelation in the knowledge of him,

If we were honest, we would say that much of what we know is teachings that came from another person and were testified or taught to us. What about revealed revelation? That is when something we know to be true from others, the Word, or the Father is revealed as truth in our hearts. This is life-changing.

I remember the revealed revelation concerning the love of the Savior and the Father towards me. I knew this to be true since the day of my conversion on September 4th, 1974. However, it was mainly a truth in my mind. I had the intellectual knowledge that the Father loved me. I read it often from God's Word. Other believers had taught and testified about the intense love of the Son and Father towards me. But in 1990, after 14 years as a believer I experienced revealed revelation within my innermost man concerning the love of God.

Many times when my boys were sick or hurt, I would say, "I would take their hurt, pain, or sickness for them if I could." Then I saw it. Before I would suffer with pain or sickness, it was in the Father's heart to suffer for me. No natural love can explain God's love. It was not that the Savor helped me in my suffering and sin. He took my place in my misery and sin. He paid a debt He did not owe because I owed a debt I could not pay.

Thought To Ponder:

Since this revealed revelation, God has captured my heart with His love. He continues to capture more of me through more of Him realized within me.

Consider This:

Father, may the eyes of my understanding continually be opened so that I really know in experience and passion what I know intellectually. Thank You, Father, for the revelation in the knowledge of You and Your glory.

-34-
DO NOT TOUCH THE HOLY THINGS

Revelation 22:8-9 (ESV) I, John, am the one who heard and saw these things. And when I heard and saw them, I fell down to worship at the feet of the angel who showed them to me, 9 but he said to me, "You must not do that! I am a fellow servant with you and your brothers the prophets, and with those who keep the words of this book. Worship God."

Sometimes, we become too familiar and complacent with spiritual things, especially the presence of God in His glory. One of the major problems in American Christianity today is an over-superfluous and flippant view of God and His manifested presence. Christians are under grace instead of the law. However, too many have completely misconstrued the teaching of grace into believing we are ultimately free to do whatever we want in some anarchy fashion, and God will forgive us anyway.

Some things we witness result from God's grace, allowing us to be partakers in His glory. They are like Peter, James, and John on the Mount of Transfiguration. They could witness the glory of the Holy things of God but were not called on to be a part of it or touch it. However, the things that the Father shows and tells us, we should shout from the rooftop unless He tells us to be still and silent.

Acts 4:19-20 (ESV) But Peter and John answered them, "Whether it is right in the sight of God to listen to you rather than to God, you must judge, 20 for we cannot but speak of what we have seen and heard."

One of the repeated themes we find throughout the Old Testament is the command not to touch the sacred things of God. There are certain places and specific objects that God calls holy and separated for Him and His purposes. Whenever anyone touched what God said not to touch, bad things happened, such as death.

The Father has made it clear that He will invite us to the places we are allowed to enter on this side of eternity. There is a presumption that we, as believers, can move into anything the Father is doing. Even the Old Testament Temple Priests knew some things were too holy to touch or enter into. By our nature, we swing from one extreme side to the other. Either we are afraid to enter into what the Father has opened before us, or we try to charge into areas that are only for us to witness His glory.

Do Not Try To Force Yourself Into The Arena That Even Angels Fear To Tread.

1 Corinthians 1:28-29 (ESV) God chose what is low and despised in the world, even things that are not, to bring to nothing things that are, 29 so that no human being might boast in the presence of God.

Thought To Ponder:

First, we must realize that if we approach God, we must be holy as God is holy. That is why we MUST appropriate the work of the cross first. Only by the blood of our Lord Jesus Christ can we be forgiven, washed clean, and allowed to touch the sacred things revealed to us. Only by the blood of Jesus can we approach the throne of God and receive His grace.

Hebrews 4:16 (ESV) Let us then with confidence draw near to the throne of grace, that we may receive mercy and find grace to help in time of need.

Consider This:

Remember, Moses and Joshua were commanded to remove their sandals because they stood on holy ground.

Father, I ask for your wisdom so that I would know what you want me to enter into and what is revealed by your grace so that I may behold your glory. Father, let me not touch the Holy things reserved for you.

-35-
NO MORE SUPERSTARS

1 Corinthians 12:12 (ESV) For just as the body is one and has many members, and all the members of the body, though many, are one body, so it is with Christ.

1 Corinthians 12:14 (ESV) For the body does not consist of one member but of many.

1 Corinthians 12:18 (ESV) But as it is, God arranged the members in the body, each one of them, as he chose.

1 Corinthians 12:21-23 (ESV) The eye cannot say to the hand, "I have no need of you," nor again the head to the feet, "I have no need of you." 22 On the contrary, the parts of the body that seem to be weaker are indispensable, 23 and on those parts of the body that we think less honorable we bestow the greater honor, and our unpresentable parts are treated with greater modesty,

In the Old Testament, God picked a man and used that man, and he became known as a mighty hero of the faith. In the New Testament, God became a man and used a people.

For many centuries, there have been spiritual superstars. Those are the individuals known throughout history that God used to reach the nations. These modern-day heroes of the faith include Billy Graham, D. L. Moody, C. S. Lewis, and the list could go on.

As we look at history, the Church has seen over and over what God could do through a yielded man or woman of God. But movements, such as the great Welsh revival, have proved what God could and wants to continue to do through the corporate body. The world longs to see the divine power manifested through groups of people and not just through a superstar. Could it be possible that the Holy Spirit wants to work through a company of believers and not just through one man or woman? What was one of the problems in the great Welsh revival when God manifested His Spirit in power and demonstration? There were many more spiritual children than moms and dads to care for them. Therefore, discipline and maturing became serious problems during the Welsh Revival.

Thought To Ponder:

We are all called to impart what we have been entrusted with. To stop the superstars from rising, we need each believer to step up to the table with their spiritual gift and use it to mature the young believers God is bringing into the house. We need a group of no-names and no-faces, just being faithful where the Father has placed them.

Consider This:

Father, may I be found faithful to do my part as a spiritual father in maturing the saints. Teach me, Lord, to teach, and may I be a fountain of blessings to others. Lord, no matter how small or seemingly insignificant my role may be, I choose to bring my part of the body into Your service.

-36-
INTERCEDING IN THE SPIRIT
PART 1

Isaiah 59:1-2 (ESV) Behold, the LORD's hand is not shortened, that it cannot save, or his ear dull, that it cannot hear; 2 but your iniquities have made a separation between you and your God, and your sins have hidden his face from you so that he does not hear.

Isaiah 59:16 (ESV) He saw that there was no man, and wondered that there was no one to intercede; then his own arm brought him salvation, and his righteousness upheld him.

Are you an intercessor? Yes, we all are called to this type of prayer ministry. It is not an isolated gift for a few "prayer warriors." Is the prayer intercession of the saints effective? Are we seeing results from our intercession? What would happen if the intercession of the Saints started with the intercession of the Holy Spirit?

The intercession we need in this evil world must be made through believers filled with the Holy Spirit. Read Is.59 for more. Many of us have felt the need and desire to be "endued with power" as promised with the Baptism of the Holy Spirit (Acts 1:8). We seem to be in the same position as the early disciples who are told to tarry until endued with power. It says that after the Holy Spirit fell in Acts 2, the disciples worshipped God and were filled with great joy. In fact, reading those early chapters of Acts, we find that they had great joy before great power. It was not until they interceded in the Spirit and spoke the things that God said that power was manifested.

Thought To Ponder:

We need power for service. We know that aimless church services and powerless and faithless prayers in the name of intercession have freed no one from bondage nor enhanced the kingdom of God. We need the Spirit of the Most High to intercede through us.

Consider This:

Father, it is your heart that we say what you say and do what you do. Forgive us for doing the religious thing when you are calling us to wait until we hear from you and then speak Your Words.

Thought To Ponder:

-37-
INTERCEDING IN THE SPIRIT
PART 2

Romans 8:26-27 (ESV) Likewise the Spirit helps us in our weakness. For we do not know what to pray for as we ought, but the Spirit himself intercedes for us with groanings too deep for words. 27 And he who searches hearts knows what is the mind of the Spirit, because the Spirit intercedes for the saints according to the will of God.

If truthful, we could acknowledge the painful reality of our prayer lives. This is not meant to condemn us but to challenge us to deep intercession.

While many of us seek words to pray, the Spirit searches the heart, mind, and spirit of both man and God to reveal and release God's heavenly destiny. Put in the same situation, what do you think we would do if we stood in front of Lazarus' tomb? What kind of exciting and bold prayer would we cast forth? What would we be saying in the Garden if we knew this was our last night to be alive? What do you think was wrong with the disciple's prayer habits and methods if they felt they had to come to Jesus and ask for prayer training in Luke 11?

Thought To Ponder:

Ezekiel 22:29-31 (ESV) The people of the land have practiced extortion and committed robbery. They have oppressed the poor and needy, and have extorted from the sojourner without justice. 30 And I sought for a man among them who should build up the wall and stand in the breach before me for the land, that I should not destroy it, but I found none. 31 Therefore I have poured out my indignation upon them. I have consumed them with the fire of my wrath. I have returned their way upon their heads, declares the Lord GOD."

Consider This:

Father, take me to places that I could not even imagine in intercession. Let me know what it really means to groan and travail until I hear from you. Make me willing to pay the price for such an honor.

-38-
IN CHRIST: A NEW MAN, YET A CHILD

Ephesians 3:17-19 (ESV) so that Christ may dwell in your hearts through faith—that you, being rooted and grounded in love, 18 may have strength to comprehend with all the saints what is the breadth and length and height and depth, 19 and to know the love of Christ that surpasses knowledge, that you may be filled with all the fullness of God.

Ephesians 4:13-14 (ESV) until we all attain to the unity of the faith and of the knowledge of the Son of God, to mature manhood, to the measure of the stature of the fullness of Christ, 14 so that we may no longer be children, tossed to and fro by the waves and carried about by every wind of doctrine, by human cunning, by craftiness in deceitful schemes.

I remember when I was a teenager, I wanted to grow up fast and be an adult. I thought all the great benefits in life came after age 21. Then it happened. One day, I woke up, and I was 21, 31, 41, 51, 61, and then 69.

Wow, I am finally a man, yet I am still a child in many ways. We all want maturity, but in the culture we live in, many times, we think things come instantly. I am a new man in Christ and have been since my conversion 31 years ago. Does that mean that I am a man and mature in everything? The more revealed revelations I see, the more I realize I am childlike in many areas. I know that I am quickened by the Spirit (Ephesians 2:1-6) and that He has raised us up to sit together in heavenly places in power. But do I really "KNOW" this? You see when our Lord was raised from the dead, the disciples beheld the Crucified Christ and the Risen Lord. But when the Holy Spirit fell in power on the Disciples, they saw the Exalted Savior and the Glorified Christ. That is the difference between a mature man and a child of the King. The child sees sins forgiven, new birthright, and eternal life. But the mature man seated in the heavenly places is endued with power and sees the Exalted Savior.

Thought To Ponder:

The Father would ask us, "Would you like to come up and sit with me"? There is room for you in the heavenly places. When we desire to be mature in this area, we will not only see the Glorified Christ but also see Him as John saw Him at Patmos (Revelation 1:1).

Consider This:

Father, I feel so inadequate at times in my knowledge of You. I really want to know what it is like to sit in the Heavenly place. Father, I cannot be satisfied with a theology about this. I want to sit before the Glorified Christ and know the Savior for more than the cross and the grave experience. I want to know Him as the Exalted Savior in fullness.

-39-
TEMPLE OF THE MOST HIGH

Romans 12:1 (ESV) I appeal to you therefore, brothers, by the mercies of God, to present your bodies as a living sacrifice, holy and acceptable to God, which is your spiritual worship.

1 Corinthians 6:19 (ESV) Or do you not know that your body is a temple of the Holy Spirit within you, whom you have from God? You are not your own,

God the Father and the Holy Spirit lived in the Son Jesus Christ. Although He was 100% human, He was also 100% God. At no time did He or could He give up His Godhood. He laid down authority and power to take up humanity, but He never ceased being God.

Jesus Christ was not born or created. He is God and has always existed with the Spirit and the Father in heaven. In the birth 2,000 years ago, God came to take on the body of man and live among men as a man and suffer and die as a man for us. God needed to work through the human body in order to redeem man. Why is all this important? God needs to live in bodies to fulfill His purposes on this earth.

For years, I have always seen God apart from flesh and blood. Then I saw He chooses and needs to dwell in the believer as His Temple on earth. In this, He has asked us for our body so that He can work through us. But for the Father to work through that body, it must belong to Him without reservation. Two people with different wills cannot serve one vision. He asks for our body and will, and He will dwell within us as GOD. For this to happen, our fallen nature must go to the cross, and He will bring His life and nature to His Temple within us.

Thought To Ponder:

Colossians 3:1-3 (ESV) If then you have been raised with Christ, seek the things that are above, where Christ is, seated at the right hand of God. 2 Set your minds on things that are above, not on things that are on earth. 3 For you have died, and your life is hidden with Christ in God.

Consider This:

Father, I am Your Temple for Your purposes. Forgive me for any area I hold back because it is Your house. May I stay cleansed and anointed for Your will and ways.

-40-
OUR SENTENCE OF DEATH

Galatians 2:20-21 (ESV) I have been crucified with Christ. It is no longer I who live, but Christ who lives in me. And the life I now live in the flesh I live by faith in the Son of God, who loved me and gave himself for me. 21 I do not nullify the grace of God, for if righteousness were through the law, then Christ died for no purpose.

When I met the Lord Jesus Christ as my Savior in 1974, I did not know anything about giving up my life as a sacrifice (Romans 12:1). Years later, as I understood the teaching, I still struggled with the thought of not having any rights because I was listed as a dead man before the Lord.

The Father clarifies that He does not want to share our lives. He wants to be Lord of all or not Lord at all. In 1990, the Father was teaching me a deeper understanding of His love and grace. It was at this time I realized that I had a sentence of death. I had lived in this body for 36 years, and how could I easily give it up? Who could decide to give up his life to another in an hour or week?

Why is it that we struggle so with death? I knew theologically that the only place for the old nature was on the cross (Romans 6), but it was not easy to go there. Then, the Father gently reminded me that He only came to take what I promised to give the Lord Jesus Christ the day I was saved. He reminded me that I said, God, I am Yours. I give my life to You.

Thought To Ponder:

Since He died for me and I have died in Him, I knew that my new life was His and not mine. I saw I would have to trust the Holy Spirit to live His life through me. Of course, I questioned the loss and delayed my answer to the Father about giving my all to Him. He was patient with me because He said, let your yes be yes, and let your no be no. In other words, be slow to make vows we do not intend to keep.

Consider This:

Father, total sacrifice is what you desire. Keep me focused that I am dead in You, and I have no rights. I don't even have the right to be right. Remind me, Father, that I don't belong to me anymore and that my life is in You.

-41-
THE ROOT OF THE NATURAL MAN

Isaiah 6:1 (ESV) In the year that King Uzziah died I saw the Lord sitting upon a throne, high and lifted up; and the train of his robe filled the temple.

Isaiah 6:5-7 (ESV) And I said: "Woe is me! For I am lost; for I am a man of unclean lips, and I dwell in the midst of a people of unclean lips; for my eyes have seen the King, the LORD of hosts!" 6 Then one of the seraphim flew to me, having in his hand a burning coal that he had taken with tongs from the altar. 7 And he touched my mouth and said: "Behold, this has touched your lips; your guilt is taken away, and your sin atoned for."

In walking daily with the Father, our goal is to conform to the image of His Son. This is not a state of doing something but a state of being something.

As we see more of our Lord's holiness, glory, and majesty, we see more of our corrupt nature. It is not that we just see the sins we commit; it is deeper than that. We see our nature destroyed by the fall of Adam.

In that old nature, we are corrupted in every way to the very core of our beings. This is not just a matter of what sins we are committing. We are guilty of all because of our nature. We don't need to be fixed. We need to be cleansed and replaced. The difference between the precious Holy Spirit and us is like the difference between light and darkness. In salvation, we have been forgiven of our sins and become a new person in our spirit man. Sin has been canceled, but what about the soulish man? It takes the Holy

Spirit's work to expose the heart's root issues. We get out of a plant what is in the root. We get out of our lives what is at the root of the heart. It is not just sin that we, as believers, are dealing with. It is now the root of self. This is why we have so much humanism within the body of Christ. Could we give consent to our heavenly Father to touch those issues of the heart that make up the self?

Thought To Ponder:

We are coming to the time and place where God is breaking the issues of our hearts forever. The place where we do not have to deal with the same heart self-issues over and over for our entire lives. AMEN! A place where the Holy Spirit takes control of areas of our lives and the root of our old nature bows to a greater authority.

Consider This:

Father, just as the seraphim took the coals from the altar and laid on the prophet's lip, we acknowledge that You are a consuming fire. Take the fire of the Holy Spirit and burn away those things that are offensive to Your Word and character. Touch my lips, Lord, and purge my heart and create a right spirit within me.

-42-
THE DIVINE NATURE

2 Peter 1:3-4 (ESV) His divine power has granted to us all things that pertain to life and godliness, through the knowledge of him who called us to his own glory and excellence, 4 by which he has granted to us his precious and very great promises, so that through them you may become partakers of the divine nature, having escaped from the corruption that is in the world because of sinful desire.

What is permissible to a new believer is not so with those seeking to be a disciple of our Lord. There is an initial surrender when we receive our Lord Jesus Christ as Savior. But as we grow, we find that the initial surrender was made without a complete understanding of a sacrificed life of service to our Father.

Step by step, the Father replaces our self-nature with His Holy Divine nature. Praise God for forgiveness of sins and the new birth. But now, the Holy Spirit desires to get to the root of the heart for replacement with His nature. He desires to deal with our ambition. This is the lust of the world.

Could We End A Ministry The Lord Has Placed In Our Hands With As Much Joy As When We Started It?

Let's read that quote again. Could we end a ministry that the Lord has placed in our hands with as much joy as we had in starting it? Could we give a successful job or ministry where we get pats on the back for a job well done to another person without jealousy?

Remember when the disciples of John the Baptist came and complained that the people were now following Jesus instead of John? John said that was why he was here, to give away his life. John the Baptist understood this truth as he gave up his reputation in his mode of dress and diet. Pleasing God was more important to him than pleasing man or himself.

Jesus says the world hated Him and would hate us. Isaiah 53 says He was despised. With our strong sense of being liked and belonging, would we be willing to be despised for the sake of following the Lord and what He says?

Thought To Ponder:

If we want to walk in the Divine nature of the Spirit, we must choose between the temporal and the eternal each day. Can we say with Abraham, Ruth, Isaiah, and many others, Lord, where you send me, I will go, and what you say I will do?

Consider This:

Father, it is an awesome privilege to be a partaker of Your divine nature and the grand promises spoken to me. Help me to desire this over the lust of the world.

-43-
WILLING TO BE MADE WILLING

Hebrews 10:19-22 (ESV) Therefore, brothers, since we have confidence to enter the holy places by the blood of Jesus, 20 by the new and living way that he opened for us through the curtain, that is, through his flesh, 21 and since we have a great priest over the house of God, 22 let us draw near with a true heart in full assurance of faith, with our hearts sprinkled clean from an evil conscience and our bodies washed with pure water.

How can "self" be willing to give up self? It is a paradox. We love ourselves. We love being first and right. We love to be recognized and appreciated. Pride is always an issue. So, what do we do about "self?"

All we do in the Christian life is tied to the will and our choices. I choose, I choose, I choose. Either I choose to remain connected to the root of my old nature or die to it and allow the Holy Spirit to replace the root with His nature.

But the paradox lies in this. How can the will of man choose to die to self? Self loves self and will do anything to protect and preserve him. But the Holy Spirit would say to us. If you are not willing, would you like me to help you? Are you willing to be made willing? The Father loves our willingness to change and be conformed to the image of His Son. Our choice of asking Him to make us ready is the right choice on our part.

Thought To Ponder:

It is the Father that gives us the victory, not our self-attempts. Our new nature allows us the boldness to exercise faith to enter boldly before His presence. Remember, no flesh will touch His glory.

Romans 7:18 (ESV) For I know that nothing good dwells in me, that is, in my flesh. For I have the desire to do what is right, but not the ability to carry it out.

Ephesians 5:17 (ESV) Therefore do not be foolish, but understand what the will of the Lord is.

Consider This:

Father, make me willing to be willing. I trust You know what I can handle better than I think I can. Therefore, I ask for Your wisdom and Your grace in this.

-44-
BEHIND THE VEIL

2 Corinthians 3:12-16 (ESV) Since we have such a hope, we are very bold, 13 not like Moses, who would put a veil over his face so that the Israelites might not gaze at the outcome of what was being brought to an end. 14 But their minds were hardened. For to this day, when they read the old covenant, that same veil remains unlifted, because only through Christ is it taken away. 15 Yes, to this day whenever Moses is read a veil lies over their hearts. 16 But when one turns to the Lord, the veil is removed.

There is a place called In the Spirit. We all desire to be In the Spirit, but what is it, and how do we do it? In the Tabernacle, a veil separated the Holy Place from the Holy of Holies. Only the High Priest could enter the Holy of Holies once a year to offer atonement for the sins of the nation. When our Lord Jesus Christ died on the cross, the veil tore from the top to the bottom, opening up the Holy of Holies, also called the Most Holy Place.

When we received the Lord Jesus Christ as our Savior, we were given grace through faith to enter boldly before the throne of God, the Holy Place. John, Paul, Peter, Isaiah, and Elijah, to name a few, were caught up in the Spirit behind the veil before the throne of God. I have been there and have talked to many others who have experienced this.

To enter into the place of heaven where the Father, Son, and the Holy Spirit dwells. After becoming a believer, the Lord calls us to obedience, practical holiness, righteousness, and a life of faith. These things allow us the joy of standing boldly before the Father in the Holiest place as the High Priest did one day a year.

Thought To Ponder:

We sing "Come Let's Go Up To The Mountain," which is the bride's cry in Song of Solomon, "Take Me To Your Chambers." Let's believe that we can not only go but also spend periods of time there.

Hebrews 6:19-20 (ESV) We have this as a sure and steadfast anchor of the soul, a hope that enters into the inner place behind the curtain, 20 where Jesus has gone as a forerunner on our behalf, having become a high priest forever after the order of Melchizedek.

Hebrews 10:19-22 (ESV) Therefore, brothers, since we have confidence to enter the holy places by the blood of Jesus, 20 by the new and living way that he opened for us through the curtain, that is, through his flesh, 21 and since we have a great priest over the house of God, 22 let us draw near with a true heart in full assurance of faith, with our hearts sprinkled clean from an evil conscience and our bodies washed with pure water.

Consider This:

Father, the veil is torn and opened by the broken flesh of our Lord Jesus Christ. May I go through the veil and stand before Your presence since I am already seated with You in the heavens.

-45-
CULTIVATING THE FALLOW GROUND

Jeremiah 4:3 (ESV) For thus says the LORD to the men of Judah and Jerusalem: "Break up your fallow ground, and sow not among thorns.

Hosea 10:12 (ESV) Sow for yourselves righteousness; reap steadfast love; break up your fallow ground, for it is the time to seek the LORD, that he may come and rain righteousness upon you.

Most of us would agree that we no longer belong to us, for we have been bought at a price. Therefore, we belong to the Lord. Well, what happens when a new owner takes possession of a property?

I have moved into many houses in my life, and all of them needed work both inside and outside. It is the same way when the Holy Spirit comes to dwell in us. There is much work to be done both inward and outward. He is not a guest or a renter. He is the new property owner, which we call our lives. God always has at least two objectives when He comes to dwell in the life of a believer. His objectives are intense cultivation and abundant fruitfulness.

Thought To Ponder:

When the land is fallow, hard, and dry from not having been plowed, the Father plows that land step by step. It is not fruitful when it is hard-hearted. Therefore, the Father plows up the fallow ground within our hearts to make room for His fruit harvest, which is His character. There is always much talk about us taking the land in some country or region. But God makes it clear that we are first to possess our own souls unto righteousness before trying to possess something outside ourselves.

1 Thessalonians 4:2-5 (ESV) For you know what instructions we gave you through the Lord Jesus. 3 For this is the will of God, your sanctification: that you abstain from sexual immorality; 4 that each one of you know how to control his own body in holiness and honor, 5 not in the passion of lust like the Gentiles who do not know God;

Consider This:

Father, teach me to be content as You plow up my life's dry, barren areas so that I may possess them as fruitful places for Your honor.

-46-
ANSWERED PRAYERS

James 5:15-16 (ESV) And the prayer of faith will save the one who is sick, and the Lord will raise him up. And if he has committed sins, he will be forgiven. 16 Therefore, confess your sins to one another and pray for one another, that you may be healed. The prayer of a righteous person has great power as it is working.

2 Corinthians 1:20 (ESV) For all the promises of God find their Yes in him. That is why it is through him that we utter our Amen to God for his glory.

We have heard that God answers prayer in three ways: yes, no, and wait. But I cannot find that in the Word. God answers true prayer with a YES!

The meaning of prayer is to communicate with God. This means that we speak, and He speaks. Prayer is not a one-way communication from us to God. If we are to express what the Father speaks, it stands to reason that we first need to hear what He is saying. So, the effectual fervent prayer of a righteous man means to pray right, pray hard, and live right simultaneously.

The answer to these prayers is always yes and AMEN. We are not only to stand in faith for the YES in these prayers but also to lose nothing to the enemy. We are also warned about losing the answer to our prayer by losing faith. When we say that effectual prayer is praying right, we mean guided prayer. We should no longer pray for all kinds of things that just pop into our heads. We are not guided when we pray whims. We need to pray for what the Holy Spirit gives us.

I believe the Father is wearied with all of our meaningless words. We must listen to the Spirit more, speak less, and only what the Father says. The things that Father gives us to speak are expensive. He has laid down the life of His Son for those things to be released. That is what it means to pray in His name. When we pray for something or someone, could we lay down our lives for that prayer request? The word fervent means mighty.

Thought To Ponder:

When we pray for what comes to us on a whim, we only pray in tongue and word. When we pray what the Holy Spirit is praying, we are praying in power, word, deed, and truth, which equals the very mind of God.

Luke 11:1 (ESV) Now Jesus was praying in a certain place, and when he finished, one of his disciples said to him, "Lord, teach us to pray, as John taught his disciples."

Consider This:

Father, I admit that much of my speaking in what I call prayer is nothing more than vain babbling. I claim Luke 11:1 for my life, Father, and ask You to teach me. Teach me to pray as John taught his disciples to pray.

-47-
TRAVAILING: LOVE IN ACTION

Isaiah 66:8 (ESV) Who has heard such a thing? Who has seen such things? Shall a land be born in one day? Shall a nation be brought forth in one moment? For as soon as Zion was in labor she brought forth her children.

Isaiah 53:10-11 (ESV) Yet it was the will of the LORD to crush him; he has put him to grief; when his soul makes an offering for guilt, he shall see his offspring; he shall prolong his days; the will of the LORD shall prosper in his hand. 11 Out of the anguish of his soul he shall see and be satisfied; by his knowledge shall the righteous one, my servant, make many to be accounted righteous, and he shall bear their iniquities.

We would say sure if we were asked if we loved "so-in-so," Mr. You Forgot His Name. But how much do we really love our brothers and sisters in the Lord? What if Mr. What's His Name got deathly sick with a disease that the doctor's report says was fatal?

We all say that we love people, especially our immediate part of the body of Christ we fellowship with, as we should. But is love free, or is love a choice and an action? Are we to love in word only or in word and deed?

What does this have to do with travailing? Travailing is a place in intercession whereby the prayer identifies with the person they are praying for. The picture in the New Testament is our Lord Jesus in the Garden praying until He sweats drops of blood. He is about to go to the cross to pay the price for our sins. The spiritual truth here is that He is standing in our place. He is about to pay a debt He did not owe for us, who owed a debt we could not pay.

In the Garden, He stood in a place for us that we could not stand at the time. He was taking the suffering and mental pain of sin upon Himself. On the cross, He stood where we could not stand in that He took all sin and physical pain and death upon Himself. He taught us how to pray in Luke 11 and John 17. In these examples, He also taught us how to travail.

Thought To Ponder:

We best understand travailing as the pain a woman goes through during childbirth. It is a pain close to death as it affects the breathing and heart rate. But in this case, travailing brings forth new life. This was the case with our Lord Jesus Christ. His travailing brought forth new life for us. If one of us got deathly sick with a disease, I hope that we would have brothers and sisters who would stand in our place in faith, prayer, and travailing. How long do we have to travail in prayer? We travail until life comes forth. Can a nation be born in a day? Yes, one life touched at a time with love, word, and deed.

Galatians 4:19 (ESV) my little children, for whom I am again in the anguish of childbirth until Christ is formed in you!

James 1:22 (ESV) But be doers of the word, and not hearers only, deceiving yourselves.

James 2:14-18 (ESV) What good is it, my brothers, if someone says he has faith but does not have works? Can that faith save him? 15 If a brother or sister is poorly clothed and lacking in daily food, 16 and one of you says to them,

"Go in peace, be warmed and filled," without giving them the things needed for the body, what good is that? 17 So also faith by itself, if it does not have works, is dead. 18 But someone will say, "You have faith and I have works." Show me your faith apart from your works, and I will show you my faith by my works.

Consider This:

Father, teach me the discipline of travailing for those whom you would have me to stand in their place of pain and suffering until life comes forth. Father, give me strength and wisdom to turn my words into action for Your glory and the building up of the saints.

-48-
KINGDOM GIVING

Luke 6:38 (ESV) give, and it will be given to you. Good measure, pressed down, shaken together, running over, will be put into your lap. For with the measure you use it will be measured back to you."

I always get a lot of questions concerning the giving of the tithe or the giving of the offering. I would like to address a principle called kingdom giving. I don't speak much about our giving money to the ministry, but it is such a kingdom thing I can't help but include it in this book.

In the Old Testament, the tithe was 10% of all that a person had and not just 10% of his income. The Tabernacle was built on nothing but the offering above the tithe. In fact, so much came in that Moses had to tell the people to stop bringing their offerings. Would it be blessed if the Church had that problem today?

I call the tithe wilderness giving or giving under the law. It is not bad, but it is just a starting place for what God had in mind for His people. In giving, we have the promise of a proportionate return in order to bless others again. This is true in everything we provide, whether it is time, service, friendship, love, or money. Our Lord's blessing proportion is 30-fold, 60-fold, 100-fold, and an open heaven to those who are faithful.

The Bible's teaching on possessions is that all we have belongs to the Lord. He owns the complete 100%, and we are just managers or stewards of what we have. This includes physical items such as our house, clothes, car, etc. But it also includes our children and our finances. I want to focus on money in this devotional because it is the most challenging area of obedience among many believers. Since my life belongs to a new owner, so does my money. In all things that I give, I receive back in direct proportion as I give. If I just "tip" God, then He will tip me.

Faithful New Testament giving is sowing beyond the tithe. The tithe is the first step of obedience. Everything after that is an offering that really tests our heart and God's Word. In the area of money, our Lord will test the reality of our surrender. We will know if faith and surrender are a reality in us when we test the Word that it is more blessed to give than to receive. If I were to ask you if you wanted an open heaven before God, you, of course, would say yes. But could we dare to test God's Word about what releases an open heaven?

Thought To Ponder:

Let me put it this way. If you are not faithful in ten or one hundred dollars before the Lord, you will not be faithful with a thousand or ten thousand.

Malachi 3:10-12 (ESV) Bring the full tithe into the storehouse, that there may be food in my house. And thereby put me to the test, says the LORD of hosts, if I will not open the windows of heaven for you and pour down for you a blessing until there is no more need. 11 I will rebuke the devourer for you, so that it will not destroy the fruits of your soil, and your vine in the field shall not fail to bear, says the LORD of hosts. 12 Then all nations will call you blessed, for you will be a land of delight, says the LORD of hosts.

2 Corinthians 9:5-8 (ESV) So I thought it necessary to urge the brothers to go on ahead to you and arrange in advance for the gift you have promised, so that it may be ready as a willing gift, not as an exaction. 6 The point is this: whoever sows sparingly will also reap sparingly, and whoever sows bountifully will also reap bountifully. 7 Each one must give as he has decided in his heart, not reluctantly or under compulsion, for God loves a cheerful giver. 8 And God is able to make all grace abound to you, so that having all sufficiency in all things at all times, you may abound in every good work.

Philippians 4:17 (ESV) Not that I seek the gift, but I seek the fruit that increases to your credit.

Consider This:

Father, You have blessed me incredibly over the years, and I rejoice with great gratitude over it. I am truly blessed, but I do not have an open heaven yet, nor do I have more than I have room for. I desire this for Your glory and a testimony to Your Word and grace. I give so I can get so that I can provide even more for the kingdom work. Teach me greater truths about kingdom giving and make me willing to obey what I know.

-49-
A COVENANT OF RITUAL OR A COVENANT OF REALITY

1 Peter 3:17-21 (ESV) For it is better to suffer for doing good, if that should be God's will, than for doing evil. 18 For Christ also suffered once for sins, the righteous for the unrighteous, that he might bring us to God, being put to death in the flesh but made alive in the spirit, 19 in which he went and proclaimed to the spirits in prison, 20 because they formerly did not obey, when God's patience waited in the days of Noah, while the ark was being prepared, in which a few, that is, eight persons, were brought safely through water. 21 Baptism, which corresponds to this, now saves you, not as a removal of dirt from the body but as an appeal to God for a good conscience, through the resurrection of Jesus Christ,

As important as water baptism is, we must understand that fulfilling the ritual of baptism is not the fulfillment of the covenant or reality of baptism. When I asked the Lord Jesus Christ to come into my life and save me, it was the start of the Covenant of Reality.

Some reject water baptism and fail to see that it represents burying the old man and raising the new man in Christ. I understood that the old Adamic nature was dead and buried through the act of receiving Christ and then being baptized. I now realized I could walk in the newness of life. I started to understand the full effect of the Covenant of Reality and the promises of God through this reality.

Far too many church members have the Covenant of Ritual. They have never been born again, and they entrust their spiritual relationship to a form of water baptism either as a baby or at some other time or event in their lives.

Some have been genuinely saved through faith in the blood cleansing of our Lord Jesus Christ, yet they have never been properly baptized. They have never entered into the Covenant of Reality. Yes, they are dead in Christ through accepting Jesus, but that is just one-half of the truth. We also need to be raised in the likeness of His resurrection.

Thought To Ponder:

When I am properly baptized, I am burying the old Adam. In coming out of the water, I walk in a good conscience through resurrection power as a new creation in Christ.

Galatians 2:20 (ESV) I have been crucified with Christ. It is no longer I who live, but Christ who lives in me. And the life I now live in the flesh I live by faith in the Son of God, who loved me and gave himself for me.

Consider This:

Father, thank You that I can walk in the newness of life since my past, the old man, is dead and buried. Thank you that I do not live or walk in my past because I no longer have a past. Thank You, Father, that Christ is being formed in me as I move from grace to grace and faith to faith.

-50-
FOREKNOWN BY THE FATHER

*Romans 8:29-30 (ESV) For those whom he **foreknew** he also **predestined** to be conformed to the image of his Son, in order that he might be the firstborn among many brothers. 30 And those whom he predestined he also **called**, and those whom he called he also **justified**, and those whom he justified he also **glorified**.*

Over the next five devotionals, we will examine the five key words in Romans 8:29-30. We see a progressive plan here in this passage of the Scriptures. We are Foreknown, Predestined, Called, Justified, and Glorified.

I do not believe in or accept the manmade doctrine of Calvinism, so don't be disappointed if I do not teach Romans 8 from that theological slant. Remember, this is a devotional and not a complex doctrinal thesis.

Foreknown means to know beforehand. It also means being acquainted with future events. Therefore, it was foreseen by God the Father all those who would believe and be saved. This supposes that there was a purpose or plan for us before the earth's foundation. This would explain what the Apostle Paul stated in Romans 8:28, that it was according to the purpose of God.

Romans 8:28 (ESV) And we know that for those who love God all things work together for good, for those who are called according to his purpose.

Romans 8:28-30 teaches that God knew us, His eyes were fixed on us, and He already saw us as being conformed to the image of His Son. In knowing us, God designated us to eternal life. We were not foreknown on account of any faith, which we could exercise, or any good works, which we would or could perform, but according to the purpose or plan of God Himself. He did not arbitrarily pick before the earth's foundations some to love Him and the rest He ignored to be eternally doomed. He is the Alpha and Omega, the beginning and the end. He is already in the infinite future and knows all things.

Thought To Ponder:

He knew me before I was born, and He already knew that I would give my life to Him on September 4th, 1974. Yes, He Foreknew me because He is all-present, past, present, and future.

I can only stand in fear, trembling, and total awe at the fact that God saw me and knew me before the heavens were spoken into existence.

Consider This:

Father, I know that Your plan will be completed in me according to Your purposes. Father, how much You know me and yet still totally love me.

-51-
PREDESTINED BY THE FATHER

*Romans 8:29-30 (ESV) For those whom he **foreknew** he also **predestined** to be conformed to the image of his Son, in order that he might be the firstborn among many brothers. 30 And those whom he predestined he also **called**, and those whom he called he also **justified**, and those whom he justified he also **glorified**.*

This is the second of five devotionals, where we will examine the five key words in Romans 8:29-30. We see a progressive plan here in this passage of the Scriptures. We are Foreknown, Predested, Called, Justified, and Glorified.

As I said in the last devotional, I do not believe in or accept the manmade doctrine of Calvinism, so don't be disappointed if I do not teach Romans 8 from that theological slant. Remember, this is a devotional and not a complex doctrinal thesis.

Predestination means to determine, purpose, or decree beforehand. We were not predestinated to the external privilege of the gospel. This means that it is not God's heart that we become saved for the benefits we experience here. All of us were predestined or determined by God to be saved and conformed to the image of His Son. However, not all people will be saved, and not all believers will be conformed to the image of His Son. Let's look at other Scriptures related to this, such as Ephesians 1:4-5 and 1:11-12.

Ephesians 1:4-5 (ESV) even as he chose us in him before the foundation of the world, that we should be holy and blameless before him. In love 5 he predestined us for adoption to himself as sons through Jesus Christ, according to the purpose of his will,

Ephesians 1:11-12 (ESV) In him we have obtained an inheritance, having been predestined according to the purpose of him who works all things according to the counsel of his will, 12 so that we who were the first to hope in Christ might be to the praise of his glory.

Thought To Ponder:

It has always been at the very heart of the Father that we become like His Son in every way. He desired this before He spoke the heavens and earth into existence.

Consider This:

Father, now I know that this is Your heartbeat. I also know that You are more committed to us being conformed to the image of Your Son than we are. Thank You, Lord, that it will be done according to Your plan and will.

-52-
CALLED BY THE FATHER

*Romans 8:29-30 (ESV) For those whom he **foreknew** he also **predestined** to be conformed to the image of his Son, in order that he might be the firstborn among many brothers. 30 And those whom he predestined he also **called**, and those whom he called he also **justified**, and those whom he justified he also **glorified**.*

This is the third of five devotionals, where we will examine the five key words in Romans 8:29-30. We see a progressive plan here in this passage of the Scriptures. We are Foreknown, Predestined, Called, Justified, and Glorified.

As I said in the last devotional, I do not believe in or accept the manmade doctrine of Calvinism, so don't be disappointed if I do not teach Romans 8 from that theological slant. Remember, this is a devotional and not a complex doctrinal thesis.

"He also called" means to be set apart by His Spirit to become believers. Before the foundation of the heavens and earth, the Father promised that He would set in motion all that would be needed for us to be romanced by the Holy Spirit.

The Father knew we would respond to His calling because He is the Alpha and Omega, the beginning and the end, and not limited by time or space. The Father did not pick a few before the foundation of the earth to be saved, and the rest are doomed to hell. By His grace, He has called all men to salvation, although all men will fail to respond to His calling.

Thought To Ponder:

What grace, what love, what patience, He has shown in that all we try to do on our own, He has determined to finish His work in us. It is a work that started before He created Adam. Yes, dear saint. Before Adam was created, God knew and called you by His name. Does this make you want to fall on your face and cry out at the awesomeness of God?

1 John 3:1 (ESV) See what kind of love the Father has given to us, that we should be called children of God; and so we are. The reason why the world does not know us is that it did not know him.

Jude 1:1-2 (ESV) Jude, a servant of Jesus Christ and brother of James, To those who are called, beloved in God the Father and kept for Jesus Christ: 2 May mercy, peace, and love be multiplied to you.

Consider This:

Father, thank You for calling me a son before I was even born. In Your infinite wisdom and Your attribute of being All-present, You saw that I would respond to Your calling. I am fearfully and wonderfully made.

-53-
JUSTIFIED BY THE FATHER

*Romans 8:29-30 (ESV) For those whom he **foreknew** he also **predestined** to be conformed to the image of his Son, in order that he might be the firstborn among many brothers. 30 And those whom he predestined he also **called**, and those whom he called he also **justified**, and those whom he justified he also **glorified**.*

This is the fourth of five devotionals, where we will examine the five key words in Romans 8:29-30. We see a progressive plan here in this passage of the Scriptures. We are Foreknown, Predestined, Called, Justified, and Glorified.

As I said in the last devotional, I do not believe in or accept the manmade doctrine of Calvinism, so don't be disappointed if I do not teach Romans 8 from that theological slant. Remember, this is a devotional and not a complex doctrinal thesis.

There is a regular order of events here. The predestination precedes the calling. The calling precedes the justification. The one is connected to the other for the purposes of God.

The purpose of God is in eternity, but our justification and glorification are in time. This means that God foreknew us by name, chose us to be conformed to the image of His Son, and called us to be Sons of the Most High. All this was done in eternity before the heavens were spoken into existence. Knowing the decisions we would make because He is not limited by time and space, God saw that we would be in Christ.

Therefore, in what we call "time," we responded to the calling of the Holy Spirit and decided for our Lord Jesus Christ, making us justified. This means we are treated as if totally righteous before the Lord. We are being regarded and treated as if we were able to keep the Law completely. Justification is by favor or grace, and not of right, but the gift of God. This is the bottom line of the gospel message. The righteousness of God is upon all who believe by faith in Jesus Christ.

Thought To Ponder:

Justification is said in simple terms. It is just as though I had never sinned. This is because Jesus took all our sins and unrighteousness.

Consider This:

Father, Thank You for our mediator, the Lord Jesus Christ, who stands before You on my behalf. You took my sins, and I took Your righteousness. Father, help me see myself justified by faith as You see me.

-54-
GLORIFIED BY THE FATHER

*Romans 8:29-30 (ESV) For those whom he **foreknew** he also **predestined** to be conformed to the image of his Son, in order that he might be the firstborn among many brothers. 30 And those whom he predestined he also **called**, and those whom he called he also **justified**, and those whom he justified he also **glorified**.*

This is the fifth and last of the devotionals, where we will examine the five key words in Romans 8:29-30. We see a progressive plan here in this passage of the Scriptures. We are Foreknown, Predestined, Called, Justified, and Glorified.

As I said in the last devotional, I do not believe in or accept the manmade doctrine of Calvinism, so don't be disappointed if I do not teach Romans 8 from that theological slant. Remember, this is a devotional and not a complex doctrinal thesis.

Glorification is when God brings us to final glory in our new bodies and the New City. We will be saved from the penalty, power, and presence of sin once and for all. Notice that all this is viewed as a past experience. This is because, starting from predestination to each of the five stages, we see successive steps of salvation unfolding in the heart of the Father.

Thought To Ponder:

All five stages combined are seen as our entire completed salvation. This will end as we share in His glory.

The power of corruption is broken in the calling, and the guilt of sin is removed in justification. All that hinders is taken out of the way, and nothing can come between our soul and God's glory. In this, God's love has its full accomplishment.

> *Romans 5:8 (ESV) but God shows his love for us in that while we were still sinners, Christ died for us.*

Consider This:

Father, by faith, I believe I will be robed in a new body as the Son of God was. By faith, I believe I have a place in the New City. By faith, I will behold Your glory.

-55-
OUR SPIRITUAL GROWTH

2 Corinthians 5:17 (ESV) Therefore, if anyone is in Christ, he is a new creation. The old has passed away; behold, the new has come.

The most exciting and important event in anyone's life is when they genuinely gave their life to the Lord Jesus Christ by faith. It is a joy knowing that we are saved and, by faith in God's Word, hold fast with confidence. But what can that assurance be based upon?

It must be more than wishful thinking. We have already stated that our assurance is based on the Word of God. But we also note that our guarantee is based on the immutability of God. He is unchanging, and His promises are yes and amen. Therefore, we can rest assured of our salvation by faith in Christ based on the Word of God, the promises of God, and the Character of God.

Let's add one more assurance for our salvation. The assurance of our salvation is also based on the Spirit of God. We walk daily with the presence of God dwelling in us in the Person of the Holy Spirit. Therefore, we are called the Temple of God.

Because He dwells in us, we are called to live in Him. As we recognize the assurances of our salvation, we start to trust the Father in more and more areas of our lives. As we trust Him more in the assurance of our salvation, we begin to dwell in His presence. In doing this, our lives start to change, taking on the Character of the Father. We are learning to dwell in Him. More and more of the old Adamic nature is put off, and the new man is put on.

Ephesians 4:22-24 (ESV) to put off your old self, which belongs to your former manner of life and is corrupt through deceitful desires, 23 and to be renewed in the spirit of your minds, 24 and to put on the new self, created after the likeness of God in true righteousness and holiness.

Thought To Ponder:

If you do not journal, you should try it. Journaling is a great way to track your spiritual growth. Somewhere, you should write this question and then answer it. "What changes have I seen in my life since I committed it to the Lordship of Jesus Christ?"

Consider This:

Father, thank You for the assurances of my salvation. Thank You for giving me confidence in my salvation based on Your Word, Promises, Character, and the indwelling Holy Spirit. Amen.

-56-
A FAITH THAT WORKS

James 2:17-18 (ESV) So also faith by itself, if it does not have works, is dead. 18 But someone will say, "You have faith and I have works." Show me your faith apart from your works, and I will show you my faith by my works.

Christianity is more than going to a building on Sunday morning, a set of religious rules, or a denominational theory. Christianity is a totally new way of life. Christianity is a faith that walks out a daily lifestyle of righteousness. It is a life of faith that brings fullness to the Christian experience. A practical Christian life is the abundant life our Lord Jesus Christ promised. A practical Christian life is Christianity at work.

We, as believers, are first called to love God with all our hearts, souls, minds, and strength. Then, we are called to love one another as we love ourselves. What do we face as believers? For one thing, we see so much selfishness, greed, hate, violence, disloyalty, and betrayal in the world today that one wonders if God's love has a chance to operate.

It is sad when we see these same worldly and immoral activities and characteristics within the Body of Christ among believers. It sometimes seems that true Christian Agape love is lost altogether among some groups of Christians.

Remember that we are called not to be a part of the world even though we are in the world. We cannot allow the selfish system of the world to crowd out the Word of God and the love of God from our hearts. If we need to be reminded of how the Word of God gets choked out of the life of a believer, we might need to reread the parable of the four soils in Matthew 13. We should pay close attention to the third soil and what happened to the plant among the thorns.

Matthew 13:22 (ESV) As for what was sown among thorns, this is the one who hears the word, but the cares of the world and the deceitfulness of riches choke the word, and it proves unfruitful.

The fact remains that God is love, and everyone who loves is born of God and knows God. Walking the love of the Father is proof that we are born again.

1 John 4:7-8 (ESV) Beloved, let us love one another, for love is from God, and whoever loves has been born of God and knows God. 8 Anyone who does not love does not know God, because God is love.

Because of this truth, we know that we can be filled with the love of God even while living in a world of hate. The first object of a Christian's love should be to God Himself. But we must remember that I do not have anything within me to love God the Father. It takes God to love God. Therefore, I must first receive His love, and then I can give back to Him what He has given me.

Thought To Ponder:

1 John 4:19 (ESV) We love because he first loved us.

We must get out of the achieving mode and into the receiving mode. We cannot work hard or long enough to deserve God's favor or love. We can only receive it by faith.

The more I receive, the more I can give back to Him and others.

Consider This:

      Father, I know You have called us to be a people of faith. We are not saved by faith and works, but we have faith that works. The evidence that our faith is at work is our love for You and our Christian brothers and sisters. Forgive us for our lack of Christian Biblical love. We choose to receive Your love even more in our hearts to be a giver of more love.

-57-
DRAWING NEAR TO THE FATHER

Mark 12:28-34 (ESV) And one of the scribes came up and heard them disputing with one another, and seeing that he answered them well, asked him, "Which commandment is the most important of all?" 29 Jesus answered, "The most important is, 'Hear, O Israel: The Lord our God, the Lord is one. 30 And you shall love the Lord your God with all your heart and with all your soul and with all your mind and with all your strength.' 31 The second is this: 'You shall love your neighbor as yourself.' There is no other commandment greater than these." 32 And the scribe said to him, "You are right, Teacher. You have truly said that he is one, and there is no other besides him. 33 And to love him with all the heart and with all the understanding and with all the strength, and to love one's neighbor as oneself, is much more than all whole burnt offerings and sacrifices." 34 And when Jesus saw that he answered wisely, he said to him, "You are not far from the kingdom of God." And after that no one dared to ask him any more questions.

If you want to shut the mouths of religious people, just start talking about loving God with all your heart, understanding, and strength. In Mark 12:28-34, we see that the conviction fell so heavily in the room that the religious crowd dared not speak another word.

As we said in the last devotional, Christianity is more than going to a building, a set of religious rules, or a denominational theory. Christianity is a new way of life. Christianity is a faith that walks out a daily lifestyle of righteousness. It is a life of faith that brings fullness to the

Christian experience. A practical Christian life is a joyful, abundant life promised in John 10:10. A practical Christian life is Christianity at work.

> *John 10:10 (ESV) The thief comes only to steal and kill and destroy. I came that they may have life and have it abundantly.*

    Today, we will look at the first discipline of Practical Christian Living, which is to love God with everything in us. We always start with loving the Father as our first object of love because it takes God to love God. We love Him because He first loved us.

    It is unthinkable that we should not love the One who has redeemed us from our sins. Actual Bible love costs. God's love for us cost the Father His only begotten Son. We should meditate on this truth and reread John 3 if our love for the Lord has grown cold.

    Nowhere does the Bible give us a more comprehensive statement concerning our relationship to our heavenly Father than the declaration of our Lord Jesus Christ in Mark 12:28-34 and Matthew 22:34-40. This makes it Biblically clear that our love for God cannot be passive but wholehearted, intense, and deeply involved in every part of our being. From these two different Bible passages, we see how we are to love our heavenly Father.

    We are to love God with our emotions.
    We are to love God with our intellect.
    We are to love God with our will.
    We are to love God with our whole physical strength.

Thought To Ponder:

Because of our love for Him, we place all that makes us up, all our powers and faculties, at His disposal. Most of us have heard or sung the song "More Love, More Power, More of You in my life." The more we learn to receive His love by faith, the better we know Him. A Christian's relationship with the Lord should be cultivated daily through prayer, studying His Word, praise, and worship time. We have the Biblical assurance that as we draw near to God, He will draw near to us.

James 4:7-8 (ESV) Submit yourselves therefore to God. Resist the devil, and he will flee from you. 8 Draw near to God, and he will draw near to you. Cleanse your hands, you sinners, and purify your hearts, you double-minded.

Hebrews 7:25 (ESV) Consequently, he is able to save to the uttermost those who draw near to God through him, since he always lives to make intercession for them.

Consider This:

Father, forgive us of any casual Christianity within us. We choose to seek You fervently and passionately. We want to be known as lovers of God more than anything else. We will prioritize our lives to seek You first in all matters, especially matters of the heart. Mode us, bend us, and shape us to be conformed to the image of Your Son, and may our love for You shine bright in a dark world.

-58-
LOVE ONE ANOTHER

Matthew 5:43-47 (ESV) "You have heard that it was said, 'You shall love your neighbor and hate your enemy.' 44 But I say to you, Love your enemies and pray for those who persecute you, 45 so that you may be sons of your Father who is in heaven. For he makes his sun rise on the evil and on the good, and sends rain on the just and on the unjust. 46 For if you love those who love you, what reward do you have? Do not even the tax collectors do the same? 47 And if you greet only your brothers, what more are you doing than others? Do not even the Gentiles do the same?

I want to remind us of some points from the last devotional before understanding the importance of loving one another. True Biblical love is not a feeling but action and obedience. Our love for God should be warm, intense, and wholehearted. The heart, soul, mind, and strength are to be deeply involved. Every part of our being is to be involved in the love process. In doing so, we place everything we are at His disposal.

Our love for God will increase as we learn to receive His love for us and our fellowship with Him deepens. A believer should build that love relationship with the Father daily through prayer, reading His Word, public and private worship, and public and personal devotions. We have God's promise in His Word that if we draw nigh to Him, He will draw near to us. As we grow in the love of God and our love for God, we will grow in all our other relationships. According to our Lord Jesus, the second greatest commandment is to "love thy neighbor as thyself."

Matthew 22:39 (ESV) And a second is like it: You shall love your neighbor as yourself.

The parable of the Good Samaritan makes it clear that our neighbor is anyone who is in need. Our lives involve constant contact with others. The typical attitude of the worldly man is to have little concern for the welfare of anyone but himself. The believer should have a different mindset. The Bible shows us that our love for God is revealed by our love for one another. Our love for one another shows the world we are His disciples.

Thought To Ponder:

John 13:34-35 (ESV) A new commandment I give to you, that you love one another: just as I have loved you, you also are to love one another. 35 By this all people will know that you are my disciples, if you have love for one another."

Consider This:

Father, as we receive and walk out Your love, we will fulfill the command to love one another. Forgive us of the selfishness that causes us to focus our time and resources on ourselves without considering others. Teach us to think of others more than ourselves. May our love for one another convict the world of their need for our Lord Jesus Christ.

-59-
BELIEVERS SHOULD NOT HURT ONE ANOTHER

Mark 12:31-34 (ESV) The second is this: 'You shall love your neighbor as yourself.' There is no other commandment greater than these." 32 And the scribe said to him, "You are right, Teacher. You have truly said that he is one, and there is no other besides him. 33 And to love him with all the heart and with all the understanding and with all the strength, and to love one's neighbor as oneself, is much more than all whole burnt offerings and sacrifices." 34 And when Jesus saw that he answered wisely, he said to him, "You are not far from the kingdom of God." And after that no one dared to ask him any more questions.

In relationships with others, we know that there are some things that love is not and does not do. True Biblical love does not demand perfection, nor does it intentionally hurt someone physically, emotionally, spiritually, financially, or relationally. We all know believers who carry their feelings around on their sleeve. They are offended easily and often. Let's look at true Biblical love from 1 Corinthians 13.

1 Corinthians 13:4-7 (ESV) Love is patient and kind; love does not envy or boast; it is not arrogant 5 or rude. It does not insist on its own way; it is not irritable or resentful; 6 it does not rejoice at wrongdoing, but rejoices with the truth. 7 Love bears all things, believes all things, hopes all things, endures all things.

Look at those words Paul penned for us concerning true Biblical love for one another. Love does not easily take offense. Love does not behave itself unseemly. Love does not manifest itself in a coarse or vulgar manner. True Biblical love gives respect to one another. The bottom line is this: believers should not hurt one another. Sadly, it is said only Christians shoot their wounded.

1 Peter 3:8-12 (ESV) Finally, all of you, have unity of mind, sympathy, brotherly love, a tender heart, and a humble mind. 9 Do not repay evil for evil or reviling for reviling, but on the contrary, bless, for to this you were called, that you may obtain a blessing. 10 For "Whoever desires to love life and see good days, let him keep his tongue from evil and his lips from speaking deceit; 11 let him turn away from evil and do good; let him seek peace and pursue it. 12 For the eyes of the Lord are on the righteous, and his ears are open to their prayer. But the face of the Lord is against those who do evil."

Remember that true love is obedience and action. Therefore, Love gives. Love is more interested in giving than in receiving. Love looks at someone and sees the best within them. When love is absent, then we see the worst within a person. Our Lord Jesus Christ looked at Peter right before his dumb statement, with the words of the enemy flowing out his mouth, and our Lord had this to say about him, "Thou art Peter, the stone." At that point and other times, Peter did not look like or act like a stone in the Body of Christ. But our Lord looked at him through eyes of love, saw what Peter would become by God's grace, and confessed those words about him.

Thought To Ponder:

The teaching about reaping what you sow is also true about love. If we want to be loved, we need to sow love. Be a person of God's love, and then we will be shown God's love in return. We will reap what we sow.

Ephesians 5:21 (ESV) submitting to one another out of reverence for Christ.

Consider This:

Father, forgive me for the times that I demanded my way, and in so doing, I left a wake of wounded bodies behind me. Remind me each day that Your love is not rude, selfish, coarse, vulgar, or easily offended, nor demands to be first, heard, and seen. May I decrease and You increase in me, so others see Christlikeness in word and deed.

-60-
LOVE YOUR ENEMIES

Matthew 5:43-47 (ESV) "You have heard that it was said, 'You shall love your neighbor and hate your enemy.' 44 But I say to you, Love your enemies and pray for those who persecute you, 45 so that you may be sons of your Father who is in heaven. For he makes his sun rise on the evil and on the good, and sends rain on the just and on the unjust. 46 For if you love those who love you, what reward do you have? Do not even the tax collectors do the same? 47 And if you greet only your brothers, what more are you doing than others? Do not even the Gentiles do the same?

Loving your enemies is the real test of God's character within the Christian. To love the lovable is no great accomplishment. Anyone can love those who love them. But the real acid test of Christianity and true Biblical love is that we love those who misuse us and do not care for us.

The first thing we must do is to identify who our enemies are according to the Word of God and not our emotions. Mentally and emotionally, we would identify our enemies as those who somehow harmed us. We could have suffered verbal, emotional, mental, physical, or spiritual attacks. It would be easy to classify those who have misused or abused us in some way as our enemies. But is this Scriptural? No. True Biblical enemies are all those who are spiritually lost and who have never received Christ as Savior. They are enemies to God, to Christ, to the work of the cross and, therefore, should be seen as our enemies. Jesus said their spiritual father is Satan. I know it is challenging to see lost family members as your enemies. However, the

Word of God classifies them as so. If you want to see how friendly they are every time you are together, tell them the gospel message.

Matthew 10:21 (ESV) Brother will deliver brother over to death, and the father his child, and children will rise against parents and have them put to death,

Matthew 10:34-37 (ESV) "Do not think that I have come to bring peace to the earth. I have not come to bring peace, but a sword. 35 For I have come to set a man against his father, and a daughter against her mother, and a daughter-in-law against her mother-in-law. 36 And a person's enemies will be those of his own household. 37 Whoever loves father or mother more than me is not worthy of me, and whoever loves son or daughter more than me is not worthy of me.

Loving our enemies is not a matter of our will but a choice to allow God's love to flow through us. We will have enemies as believers. Our Lord Jesus Christ says if the world hated Him, how much more will the world hate us? The world is identified as those who do not know Christ.

John 15:18-20 (ESV) "If the world hates you, know that it has hated me before it hated you. 19 If you were of the world, the world would love you as its own; but because you are not of the world, but I chose you out of the world, therefore the world hates you. 20 Remember the word that I said to you: 'A servant is not greater than his master.' If they persecuted me, they will also persecute you. If they kept my word, they will also keep yours.

Then He says, woe to them whom the world speaks well of. So, how should we act when our enemies persecute us? We are called on by the Father to love them. But that is not our only action of obedience.

Luke 6:22-23 (ESV) "Blessed are you when people hate you and when they exclude you and revile you and spurn your name as evil, on account of the Son of Man! 23 Rejoice in that day, and leap for joy, for behold, your reward is great in heaven; for so their fathers did to the prophets.

Thought To Ponder:

Our love for God will give us the confidence and assurance that we can leap for joy. Remember that God the Father sets our table in the presence of our enemies (Psalms 23). Know that our testimony to a lost and dying world will make many uncomfortable and cause many to become enemies. Our Lord Jesus Christ set the example for us. He always did the good and right thing, yet we find Him hated more than anyone of His day. In the height of man's hatred, our Lord Jesus Christ spoke these words from the cross, "Father, forgive them, for they know not what they do."

Consider This:

Father, we forgive our enemies, for they do not know what they are doing. Yes, we have been hurt. Yes, we will be hurt. However, we choose not to let our hurt define us as wounded survivors. We are overcomers and more than conquerors. We will choose to obey Your Word and leap for joy. Bless You, Lord. Amen and Amen!

MORE BOOKS BY CHARLES MORRIS

1. The Four Positions Of The Holy Spirit
2. Born Again
3. The 10 Characteristics Of A Spirit-Filled Church
4. The Covenant Of Salt
5. The Parable Of The Four Soils
6. The Five Evidences Of Salvation
7. Hosea
8. Preparing Ourselves To Hear The Voice Of God
9. Fifteen Ways To Hear The Voice Of God
10. The 24 Qualifications Of An Elder
11. The Bible Proves Itself True
12. Experiencing The Beauty Of Brokenness
13. Places Where God And Man Meet
14. Your Dash
15. Chart Your Path
16. The Five Witnesses Of Salvation
17. How Do I Write A Book?
18. Hosea Introduction
19. Hosea 1:1-3
20. Hosea 1:4-5
21. Hosea 1:6-7
22. Hosea 1:8-9
23. Hosea 1:10-11
24. A Willingness To Be Taught
25. Luke 15
26. The Chronological Book Of End Times
27. Is Atheism Dead?
28. Wherever You Go Travel Journal Adults
29. Wherever You Go Travel Journal Teens
30. The Topical Journal Veterans
31. The Topical Journal Women
32. The Topical Journal Adults
33. Wherever You Go Travel Journal Men

34. The Topical Journal Men
35. Is Religion Dead?
36. Unleashed
37. I Feel Like I'm Losing My Faith
38. We Need Faith
39. Is Christian Immaturity Dead?
40. The Parable Of The Wheat And Tares
41. Go Tell It On The Mountain
42. The Cost Of Discipleship
43. The Power Of One More
44. The Gospel According To Luke
45. The Gospel According To Jesus
46. I Am Light & Dark Blue, Light & Dark Pink, Gold & Peach
47. Devotional Bible Series Volume 3: Six Enemies Of Faith
48. Devotional Bible Series Volume 5: Intimate Deception: What Are The Six Dangerous Love Affairs?
49. Overcoming Fear
50. Don't Give The Enemy A Seat At Your Table
51. A Course In Miracles
52. Angels
53. The Holy Spirit; Do I Have To Speak In Tongues?
54. Host The Holy Ghost
55. Devotional Bible Series Volume 1: Defeating The Sin Within Me
56. Devotional Bible Series Volume 2: A Backsliding Heart
57. Devotional Bible Series Volume 4: The Spiritual Man
58. Devotional Bible Series Volume 6: Setting Your Heart
59. Devotional Bible Series Volume 7: Dare To Pray

ABOUT THE AUTHOR

CHARLES MORRIS has a rich legacy spanning 49 years as a dedicated servant of God to the body of Christ. His diverse roles as a pastor, church planter, evangelist, house church coordinator, and prolific author of over 50 books have left a profound impact on countless lives.

As the visionary founder and CEO of RSI Ministry and Raising the Standard International Publishing, Pastor Charles remains committed to inspiring believers to walk in God's holiness through the power and presence of the Holy Spirit.

Passionate about living according to God's standards, he tirelessly calls the church to embody Christ's likeness in their daily lives in word, deed, and thought. Pastor Charles firmly believes in the significance of genuine salvation, encouraging all believers to examine their lives through the lens of God's Word.

Currently residing in Navarre, Florida, Pastor Charles finds unwavering support and partnership in life with his beloved wife, Debra.

Made in the USA
Monee, IL
15 February 2024

3c699076-2cdb-42bf-bdef-069e197f3059R01